NINE ONE-ACT PLAYS

MACMILLAN AND CO., Limited
LONDON · BOMBAY · CALCUTTA · MADRAS
MELBOURNE

THE MACMILLAN COMPANY
NEW YORK · BOSTON · CHICAGO
DALLAS · ATLANTA · SAN FRANCISCO

THE MACMILLAN COMPANY
OF CANADA, LIMITED
TORONTO

NINE ONE-ACT PLAYS

By

W. B. YEATS

MACMILLAN AND CO., LIMITED
ST. MARTIN'S STREET, LONDON
1937

NOTE

Those who are interested in the music for use in the performance of *Cathleen ni Houlihan*, *The Hour-Glass*, *The Pot of Broth*, *On Baile's Strand*, and *Deirdre* will find it reproduced at the end of the volume of *Plays in Prose and Verse* in the Collected Edition of the author's works (Macmillan. 10s. 6d. net).

Application for the right of performing these plays or of reading them in public should be made to Messrs. Samuel French, Ltd., 26 Southampton Street, London, W.C.2.

CONTENTS

THE LAND OF HEART'S DESIRE

1894

'O Rose, thou art sick'

William Blake

TO
FLORENCE FARR

THE LAND OF HEART'S DESIRE

PERSONS IN THE PLAY

Maurteen Bruin	Mary Bruin
Bridget Bruin	Father Hart
Shawn Bruin	A Faery Child

The Scene is laid in the Barony of Kilmacowen, in the County of Sligo, and at a remote time

A room with a hearth on the floor in the middle of a deep alcove to the right. There are benches in the alcove and a table; and a crucifix on the wall. The alcove is full of a glow of light from the fire. There is an open door facing the audience to the left, and to the left of this a bench. Through the door one can see the forest. It is night, but the moon or a late sunset glimmers through the trees and carries the eye far off into a vague, mysterious world. Maurteen Bruin, Shawn Bruin, and Bridget Bruin sit in the alcove at the table or about the fire. They are dressed in the costume of some remote time, and near them sits an old priest, Father Hart. He may be dressed as a friar. There is food and drink upon the table. Mary Bruin stands by the door reading a book. If she looks up she can see through the door into the wood.

Bridget. Because I bid her clean the pots for supper
    She took that old book down out of the thatch;
    She has been doubled over it ever since.
    We should be deafened by her groans and moans
    Had she to work as some do, Father Hart;

Get up at dawn like me and mend and scour
Or ride abroad in the boisterous night like you,
The pyx and blessed bread under your arm.

Shawn. Mother, you are too cross.

Bridget.   You've married her,
And fear to vex her and so take her part.

Maurteen [*to Father Hart*]. It is but right that youth
        should side with youth;
She quarrels with my wife a bit at times,
And is too deep just now in the old book!
But do not blame her greatly; (she will grow
As quiet as a puff-ball in a tree
When but the moons of marriage dawn and die
For half a score of times.) [1]

Father Hart.   Their hearts are wild,
As be the hearts of birds, till children come.

Bridget. She would not mind the kettle, milk the cow,
Or even lay the knives and spread the cloth.

Shawn. Mother, if only——

Maurteen.   Shawn, this is half empty;
Go, bring up the best bottle that we have.

Father Hart. I never saw her read a book before,
What can it be?

Maurteen [*to Shawn*]. What are you waiting for?
You must not shake it when you draw the cork;
It's precious wine, so take your time about it.
                                    [*Shawn goes.*

---

[1] Amateurs perform this more often than any other play of
mine, and I urge them to omit all lines that I have enclosed in
heavy round brackets ( ).—W. B. Y.

[*To Priest.*] (There was a Spaniard wrecked at Ocris
    Head,
When I was young, and I have still some bottles.)
He cannot bear to hear her blamed; the book
Has lain up in the thatch these fifty years;
My father told me my grandfather wrote it,
And killed a heifer for the binding of it—
(But supper's spread, and we can talk and eat)
It was little good he got out of the book,
Because it filled his house with rambling fiddlers,
And rambling ballad-makers and the like.
(The griddle-bread is there in front of you.)
Colleen, what is the wonder in that book,
That you must leave the bread to cool? Had I
Or had my father read or written books
There were no stocking stuffed with yellow guineas
To come when I am dead to Shawn and you.

Father Hart. You should not fill your head with foolish
    dreams.
    What are you reading?

Mary.   How a Princess Edain,
    A daughter of a King of Ireland, heard
    A voice singing on a May Eve like this,
    And followed, half awake and half asleep,
    Until she came into the Land of Faery,
    Where nobody gets old and godly and grave,
    Where nobody gets old and crafty and wise,
    Where nobody gets old and bitter of tongue.
    And she is still there, busied with a dance
    Deep in the dewy shadow of a wood,
    (Or where stars walk upon a mountain-top.)

Maurteen. Persuade the colleen to put down the book;

My grandfather would mutter just such things,
And he was no judge of a dog or a horse,
And any idle boy could blarney him;
Just speak your mind.

Father Hart.   Put it away, my colleen;
(God spreads the heavens above us like great wings
And gives a little round of deeds and days,
And then come the wrecked angels and set snares,
And bait them with light hopes and heavy dreams,
Until the heart is puffed with pride and goes
Half shuddering and half joyous from God's peace;)
For it was some wrecked angel, blind with tears,
Who flattered Edain's heart with merry words.
My colleen, I have seen some other girls
Restless and ill at ease, but years went by
And they grew like their neighbours and were glad
In minding children, working at the churn,
And gossiping of weddings and of wakes;
(For life moves out of a red flare of dreams
Into a common light of common hours,
Until old age bring the red flare again.)

Maurteen. That's true—but she's too young to know
it's true.

Bridget. She's old enough to know that it is wrong
To mope and idle.

Maurteen.   I've little blame for her;
She's dull when my big son is in the fields,
And that and maybe this good woman's tongue
Have driven her to hide among her dreams
Like children from the dark under the bedclothes.

Bridget. She'd never do a turn if I were silent.

Maurteen. And maybe it is natural upon May Eve

To dream of the Good People. But tell me, girl,
If you've the branch of blessed quicken wood
That women hang upon the post of the door
That they may send good luck into the house?
Remember they may steal new-married brides
After the fall of twilight on May Eve,
Or what old women mutter at the fire
Is but a pack of lies.

Father Hart.　　　　　It may be truth.
We do not know the limit of those powers
God has permitted to the evil spirits
For some mysterious end. You have done right [*to
　　Mary*];
It's well to keep old innocent customs up.
　　[*Mary Bruin has taken a bough of quicken wood from a
　　seat and hung it on a nail in the door-post. A girl
　　child strangely dressed, perhaps in faery green, comes
　　out of the wood and takes it away.*

Mary. I had no sooner hung it on the nail
Before a child ran up out of the wind;
She has caught it in her hand and fondled it;
(Her face is pale as water before dawn.)

Father Hart. Whose child can this be?

Maurteen.　　　　　No one's child at all.
She often dreams that some one has gone by,
When there was nothing but a puff of wind.

Mary. They have taken away the blessed quicken wood,
They will not bring good luck into the house;
Yet I am glad that I was courteous to them,
For are not they, likewise, children of God?

Father Hart. Colleen, they are the children of the Fiend,

And they have power until the end of time,
When God shall fight with them a great pitched
    battle
And hack them into pieces.

Mary.   He will smile,
    Father, perhaps, and open His great door.

Father Hart. Did but the lawless angels see that door
    They would fall, slain by everlasting peace;
    And when such angels knock upon our doors,
    Who goes with them must drive through the same
        storm.
    [*An arm comes round the door-post and knocks and
    beckons. It is clearly seen in the silvery light. Mary
    Bruin goes to door and stands in it for a moment.
    Maurteen Bruin is busy filling Father Hart's plate.
    Bridget Bruin stirs the fire.*

Mary [*coming to table*]. There's somebody out there that
        beckoned me
    And raised her hand as though it held a cup,
    And she was drinking from it, so it may be
    That she is thirsty.
    [*She takes milk from the table and carries it to the door.*

Father Hart.   That will be the child
    That you would have it was no child at all.
Bridget. (And maybe, Father, what he said was true;
    For there is not another night in the year
    So wicked as to-night.

Maurteen.   Nothing can harm us
    While the good Father's underneath our roof.

Mary. A little queer old woman dressed in green.

Bridget. The Good People beg for milk and fire

Upon May Eve—woe to the house that gives,
For they have power upon it for a year.

Maurteen. Hush, woman, hush!

Bridget. She's given milk away.
I knew she would bring evil on the house.

Maurteen. Who was it?

Mary. Both the tongue and face were strange.

Maurteen. Some strangers came last week to Clover
Hill;
She must be one of them.)

Bridget. I am afraid.

Father Hart. The Cross will keep all evil from the
house
While it hangs there.

Maurteen. Come, sit beside me, colleen,
And put away your dreams of discontent,
For I would have you light up my last days,
Like the good glow of the turf; and when I die
You'll be the wealthiest hereabout, for, colleen,
I have a stocking full of yellow guineas
Hidden away where nobody can find it.

Bridget. You are the fool of every pretty face,
And I must spare and pinch that my son's wife
May have all kinds of ribbons for her head.

Maurteen. Do not be cross; she is a right good girl!
(The butter is by your elbow, Father Hart.
My colleen, have not Fate and Time and Change
Done well for me and for old Bridget there?)
We have a hundred acres of good land,
And sit beside each other at the fire.

I have this reverend Father for my friend,
I look upon your face and my son's face—
We've put his plate by yours—and here he comes,
And brings with him the only thing we have lacked,
Abundance of good wine. [*Shawn comes in.*] Stir up
    the fire,
And put new turf upon it till it blaze;
To watch the turf-smoke coiling from the fire,
And feel content and wisdom in your heart,
This is the best of life; (when we are young
We long to tread a way none trod before,
But find the excellent old way through love,
And through the care of children, to the hour
For bidding Fate and Time and Change good-bye.)
    [*Mary stands for a moment in the door (and then takes
    a sod of turf from the fire and goes out through the
    door. Shawn follows her and meets her coming in.*)

Shawn. What is it draws you to the chill o' the wood?
    There is a light among the stems of the trees
    That makes one shiver.

Mary.   A little queer old man
    Made me a sign to show he wanted fire
    To light his pipe.

Bridget.   You've given milk and fire
    Upon the unluckiest night of the year and brought,
    For all you know, evil upon the house.
    Before you married you were idle and fine
    And went about with ribbons on your head;
    And now—no, Father, I will speak my mind—
    She is not a fitting wife for any man——

Shawn. Be quiet, mother!

Maurteen.   You are much too cross.

Mary. What do I care if I have given this house,
Where I must hear all day a bitter tongue,
Into the power of faeries!

Bridget. You know well
How calling the Good People by that name,
Or talking of them over-much at all,
May bring all kinds of evil on the house.

Mary. Come, faeries, take me out of this dull house!
Let me have all the freedom I have lost;
Work when I will and idle when I will!
Faeries, come take me out of this dull world,
For I would ride with you upon the wind,
(Run on the top of the dishevelled tide,)
And dance upon the mountains like a flame.

Father Hart. You cannot know the meaning of your
words.

Mary. Father, I am right weary of four tongues:
A tongue that is too crafty and too wise,
A tongue that is too godly and too grave,
A tongue that is more bitter than the tide,
And a kind tongue too full of drowsy love,
Of drowsy love and my captivity.

[*Shawn Bruin leads her to a seat at the left of the door.*

Shawn. Do not blame me; I often lie awake
Thinking that all things trouble your bright head.
How beautiful it is—your broad pale forehead
Under a cloudy blossoming of hair!
Sit down beside me here—these are too old,
And have forgotten they were ever young.

Mary. O, you are the great door-post of this house,
And I the branch of blessed quicken wood,
And if I could I'd hang upon the post

B

Till I had brought good luck into the house.
   [*She would put her arms about him, but looks shyly at
   the priest and lets her arms fall.*

Father Hart. My daughter, take his hand—by love alone
   God binds us to Himself and to the hearth,
   That shuts us from the waste beyond His peace,
   From maddening freedom and bewildering light.

Shawn. Would that the world were mine to give it you,
   And not its quiet hearths alone, but even
   All that bewilderment of light and freedom,
   If you would have it.

Mary.   I would take the world
   And break it into pieces in my hands
   To see you smile watching it crumble away.

Shawn. Then I would mould a world of fire and dew,
   With no one bitter, grave or over-wise,
   And nothing marred or old to do you wrong,
   And crowd the enraptured quiet of the sky
   With candles burning to your lonely face.

Mary. Your looks are all the candles that I need.

Shawn. Once a fly dancing in a beam of the sun,
   Or the light wind blowing out of the dawn,
   Could fill your heart with dreams none other knew,
   But now the indissoluble sacrament
   Has mixed your heart that was most proud and cold
   With my warm heart for ever; the sun and moon
   Must fade and heaven be rolled up like a scroll,
   But your white spirit still walk by my spirit.
                     [*A Voice singing in the wood.*

Maurteen. There's some one singing. Why, it's but a
   child.

It sang, 'The lonely of heart is withered away.'
A strange song for a child, but she sings sweetly.
Listen, listen!   [*Goes to door.*

Mary.   O, cling close to me,
Because I have said wicked things to-night.

The Voice. The wind blows out of the gates of the day,
The wind blows over the lonely of heart,
And the lonely of heart is withered away.
While the faeries dance in a place apart,
Shaking their milk-white feet in a ring,
Tossing their milk-white arms in the air;
For they hear the wind laugh and murmur and sing
Of a land where even the old are fair,
And even the wise are merry of tongue;
But I heard a reed of Coolaney say,
'When the wind has laughed and murmured and
    sung
The lonely of heart is withered away!'

Maurteen. Being happy, I would have all others happy,
So I will bring her in out of the cold.
                         [*He brings in the faery child.*

The Child. (I tire of winds and waters and pale lights.

Maurteen. And that's no wonder, for when night has
    fallen)
The wood's a cold and a bewildering place,
But you are welcome here.

The Child.   I am welcome here.
(But when I tire of this warm little house)
There is one here that must away, away.

Maurteen. O, listen to her dreamy and strange talk.
Are you not cold?

The Child.   I will crouch down beside you,
  For I have run a long, long way this night.

Bridget. You have a comely shape.

Maurteen.   Your hair is wet.

Bridget. I'll warm your chilly feet.

Maurteen.   You have come indeed
  A long, long way—for I have never seen
  Your pretty face—and must be tired and hungry.
  Here is some bread and wine.

The Child.   The wine is bitter.
  Old mother, have you no sweet food for me?

Bridget. I have some honey.   [*She goes into the next room.*

Maurteen.   You have coaxing ways.
  The mother was quite cross before you came.
    [*Bridget returns with the honey and fills a porringer with
    milk.*

Bridget. She is the child of gentle people; look
  At her white hands and at her pretty dress.
  I've brought you some new milk, but wait a while
  And I will put it to the fire to warm,
  For things well fitted for poor folk like us
  Would never please a high-born child like you.

The Child. From dawn, when you must blow the fire
    ablaze,
  You work your fingers to the bone, old mother.
  The young may lie in bed and dream and hope,
  But you must work your fingers to the bone
  Because your heart is old.

Bridget.   The young are idle.

The Child. Your memories have made you wise, old
    father;
  The young must sigh through many a dream and
    hope,
  But you are wise because your heart is old.
                 [*Bridget gives her more bread and honey.*

Maurteen. O, who would think to find so young a girl
  Loving old age and wisdom?

The Child.   No more, mother.

Maurteen. What a small bite! The milk is ready now.
                        [*Hands it to her.*
  What a small sip!

The Child.   Put on my shoes, old mother.
  For I would like to dance now I have eaten.
  The reeds are dancing by Coolaney lake,
  And I would like to dance until the reeds
  And the white waves have danced themselves asleep.
    [*Bridget puts on the shoes, and the Child is about to
    dance, but suddenly sees the crucifix and shrieks and
    covers her eyes.*
  What is that ugly thing on the black cross?

Father Hart. You cannot know how naughty your words
    are!
  That is our Blessed Lord.

The Child.   Hide it away!

Bridget. I have begun to be afraid again.

The Child. Hide it away!

Maurteen.   That would be wickedness!

Bridget. That would be sacrilege!

The Child.   The tortured thing!
  Hide it away!

Maurteen.   Her parents are to blame.

Father Hart. That is the image of the Son of God.

The Child [*caressing him*]. Hide it away, hide it away!

Maurteen.   No, no.

Father Hart. Because you are so young and like a bird,
  That must take fright at every stir of the leaves,
  I will go take it down.

The Child.   Hide it away!
  And cover it out of sight and out of mind!
    [*Father Hart takes crucifix from wall and carries it to-
      wards inner room.*

Father Hart. Since you have come into this barony,
  I will instruct you in our blessed Faith;
  And being so keen-witted you'll soon learn.
                              [*To the others.*]
  We must be tender to all budding things.
  Our Maker let no thought of Calvary
  Trouble the morning stars in their first song.
                      [*Puts crucifix in inner room.*

The Child. Here is level ground for dancing; I will
  dance.
                    [*Sings*]
  The wind blows out of the gates of the day,
  The wind blows over the lonely of heart,
  And the lonely of heart is withered away.
                      [*She dances.*

Mary [*to Shawn*]. Just now when she came near I thought
    I heard
  Other small steps beating upon the floor,

And a faint music blowing in the wind,
Invisible pipes giving her feet the tune.

Shawn. I heard no steps but hers.

Mary.   I hear them now.
The unholy powers are dancing in the house.

Maurteen. Come over here, and if you promise me
Not to talk wickedly of holy things
I will give you something.

The Child.   Bring it me, old father.

Maurteen. Here are some ribbons that I bought in the
town
For my son's wife—but she will let me give them
To tie up that wild hair the winds have tumbled.

The Child. Come, tell me, do you love me?

Maurteen.   Yes, I love you.

The Child. Ah, but you love this fireside. Do you love
me?

Father Hart. When the Almighty puts so great a share
Of His own ageless youth into a creature,
To look is but to love.

The Child.   But you love Him?

Bridget. She is blaspheming.

The Child.   And do you love me too?

Mary. I do not know.

The Child.   You love that young man there,
Yet I could make you ride upon the winds,
(Run on the top of the dishevelled tide,)
And dance upon the mountains like a flame.

Mary. Queen of Angels and kind saints defend us!

Some dreadful thing will happen. A while ago
She took away the blessed quicken wood.

Father Hart. You fear because of her unmeasured prattle;
She knows no better. Child, how old are you?

The Child. When winter sleep is abroad my hair grows thin,
My feet unsteady. When the leaves awaken
My mother carries me in her golden arms.
I'll soon put on my womanhood and marry
The spirits of wood and water, but who can tell
When I was born for the first time? I think
I am much older than the eagle-cock
(That blinks and blinks on Ballygawley Hill,)
And he is the oldest thing under the moon.

Father Hart. O, she is of the faery people.

The Child.   One called.
I sent my messengers for milk and fire;
She called again and after that I came.
    [*All except Shawn and Mary Bruin gather behind the
    priest for protection.*

Shawn [*rising*]. Though you have made all these obedient,
You have not charmed my sight and won from me
A wish or gift to make you powerful;
I'll turn you from the house.

Father Hart.   No, I will face her.

The Child. Because you took away the crucifix
I am so mighty that there's none can pass,
Unless I will it, where my feet have danced
Or where I've whirled my finger-tips.
                    [*Shawn tries to approach her and cannot.*

Maurteen.   Look, look!
  There something stops him—look how he moves his
      hands
  As though he rubbed them on a wall of glass!

Father Hart. I will confront this mighty spirit alone;
  Put fear away; the Father is with us,
  (The Holy Martyrs and the Innocents,
  The adoring Magi in their coats of mail,)
  And He who died and rose on the third day,
  (And all the nine angelic hierarchies.)
    [*The Child kneels upon the settle beside Mary and puts
    her arms about her.*
  Cry, daughter, to the Angels and the Saints.

The Child. You shall go with me, newly-married bride,
  And gaze upon a merrier multitude.
  (White-armed Nuala, Aengus of the Birds,
  Feacra of the hurtling foam, and him
  Who is the ruler of the Western Host,
  Finvaragh, and their Land of Heart's Desire,)
  Where beauty has no ebb, decay no flood,
  But joy is wisdom, time an endless song.
  I kiss you and the world begins to fade.

Shawn. Awake out of that trance—and cover up
  Your eyes and ears.

Father Hart.   She must both look and listen,
  For only the soul's choice can save her now.
  Come over to me, daughter; stand beside me;
  Think of this house and of your duties in it.

The Child. Stay and come with me, newly-married
      bride,
  For if you hear him you grow like the rest;

Bear children, cook, and bend above the churn,
And wrangle over butter, fowl, and eggs,
Until at last, grown old and bitter of tongue,
You're crouching there and shivering at the grave.

Father Hart. Daughter, I point you out the way to
Heaven.

The Child. But I can lead you, newly-married bride,
Where nobody gets old and crafty and wise,
Where nobody gets old and godly and grave,
Where nobody gets old and bitter of tongue,
And where kind tongues bring no captivity;
For we are but obedient to the thoughts
That drift into the mind at a wink of the eye.

Father Hart. By the dear Name of the One crucified,
I bid you, Mary Bruin, come to me.

The Child. I keep you in the name of your own heart.

Father Hart. It is because I put away the crucifix
That I am nothing, and my power is nothing.
I'll bring it here again.

Maurteen [*clinging to him*]. No.

Bridget.   Do not leave us.

Father Hart. O, let me go before it is too late;
It is my sin alone that brought it all.

                                    [*Singing outside.*

The Child. I hear them sing, 'Come, newly-married
bride,
Come to the woods and waters and pale lights.'

Mary. I will go with you.

Father Hart.   She is lost, alas!

The Child [*standing by the door*]. But clinging mortal hope
    must fall from you,
  For we who ride the winds, run on the waves,
  And dance upon the mountains are more light
  Than dewdrops on the banner of the dawn.

Mary. O, take me with you.

Shawn.   Beloved, I will keep you.
  I've more than words, I have these arms to hold you,
  Nor all the faery host, do what they please,
  Shall ever make me loose you from these arms.

Mary. Dear face! Dear voice!

The Child.   Come, newly-married bride.

Mary. I always loved her world—and yet—and yet——

The Child. White bird, white bird, come with me, little
    bird.

Mary. She calls me!

The Child.   Come, come with me, little bird.
           [*Distant dancing figures appear in the wood.*

Mary. I can hear songs and dancing.

Shawn.   Stay with me.

Mary. I think that I would stay—and yet—and yet——

The Child. Come, little bird with crest of gold.

Mary [*very softly*].   And yet——

The Child. Come, little bird with silver feet!
        [*Mary Bruin dies, and the Child goes.*

Shawn.   She is dead!

Bridget. Come from that image; body and soul are gone.
  You have thrown your arms about a drift of leaves,
  Or bole of an ash-tree changed into her image.

Father Hart. Thus do the spirits of evil snatch their
  prey
  Almost out of the very hand of God;
  And day by day their power is more and more,
  And men and women leave old paths, for pride
  Comes knocking with thin knuckles on the heart.

[*Outside there are dancing figures, and it may be a white bird,
  and many voices singing:*
  The wind blows out of the gates of the day,
  The wind blows over the lonely of heart,
  And the lonely of heart is withered away;
  (While the faeries dance in a place apart,
  Shaking their milk-white feet in a ring,
  Tossing their milk-white arms in the air;
  For they hear the wind laugh and murmur and sing
  Of a land where even the old are fair,
  And even the wise are merry of tongue;
  But I heard a reed of Coolaney say—
  'When the wind has laughed and murmured and
    sung,
  The lonely of heart is withered away.')

THE END

CATHLEEN NI HOULIHAN

1902

CATHLEEN NI HOULIHAN

PERSONS IN THE PLAY

Peter Gillane
Michael Gillane, *his son, going to be married*
Patrick Gillane, *a lad of twelve, Michael's brother*

Bridget Gillane, *Peter's wife*
Delia Cahel, *engaged to Michae*
The Poor Old Woman
Neighbours

Interior of a cottage close to Killala, in 1798. Bridget is standing at a table undoing a parcel. Peter is sitting at one side of the fire, Patrick at the other.

Peter. What is that sound I hear?

Patrick. I don't hear anything. [*He listens.*] I hear it now. It's like cheering. [*He goes to the window and looks out.*] I wonder what they are cheering about. I don't see anybody.

Peter. It might be a hurling.

Patrick. There's no hurling to-day. It must be down in the town the cheering is.

Bridget. I suppose the boys must be having some sport of their own. Come over here, Peter, and look at Michael's wedding clothes.

Peter [*shifts his chair to table*]. Those are grand clothes, indeed.

Bridget. You hadn't clothes like that when you married me, and no coat to put on of a Sunday more than any other day.

Peter. That is true, indeed. We never thought a son of our own would be wearing a suit of that sort for his wedding, or have so good a place to bring a wife to.

Patrick [*who is still at the window*]. There's an old woman coming down the road. I don't know is it here she is coming.

Bridget. It will be a neighbour coming to hear about Michael's wedding. Can you see who it is?

Patrick. I think it is a stranger, but she's not coming to the house. She's turned into the gap that goes down where Maurteen and his sons are shearing sheep. [*He turns towards Bridget.*] Do you remember what Winny of the Cross Roads was saying the other night about the strange woman that goes through the country whatever time there's war or trouble coming?

Bridget. Don't be bothering us about Winny's talk, but go and open the door for your brother. I hear him coming up the path.

Peter. I hope he has brought Delia's fortune with him safe, for fear the people might go back on the bargain and I after making it. Trouble enough I had making it.
[*Patrick opens the door and Michael comes in.*

Bridget. What kept you, Michael? We were looking out for you this long time.

Michael. I went round by the priest's house to bid him be ready to marry us to-morrow.

Bridget. Did he say anything?

Michael. He said it was a very nice match, and that he was never better pleased to marry any two in his parish than myself and Delia Cahel.

Peter. Have you got the fortune, Michael?

Michael. Here it is.
[*Michael puts bag on table and goes over and leans against chimney-jamb. Bridget, who has been all this time examining the clothes, pulling the seams and trying the lining of the pockets, etc., puts the clothes on the dresser.*

Peter [*getting up and taking the bag in his hand and turning out the money*]. Yes, I made the bargain well for you, Michael. Old John Cahel would sooner have kept a share of this a while longer. 'Let me keep the half of it until the first boy is born,' says he. 'You will not,' says I. 'Whether there is or is not a boy, the whole hundred pounds must be in Michael's hands before he brings your daughter to the house.' The wife spoke to him then, and he gave in at the end.

Bridget. You seem well pleased to be handling the money, Peter.

Peter. Indeed, I wish I had had the luck to get a hundred pounds, or twenty pounds itself, with the wife I married.

Bridget. Well, if I didn't bring much I didn't get much. What had you the day I married you but a flock of hens and you feeding them, and a few lambs and you driving them to the market at Ballina? [*She is vexed and bangs a jug on the dresser.*] If I brought no fortune I worked it out in my bones, laying down the baby, Michael that is standing there now, on a stook of straw, while I dug the potatoes, and never asking big dresses or anything but to be working.

Peter. That is true, indeed.   [*He pats her arm.*

C

Bridget. Leave me alone now till I ready the house for the woman that is to come into it.

Peter. You are the best woman in Ireland, but money is good, too. [*He begins handling the money again and sits down.*] I never thought to see so much money within my four walls. We can do great things now we have it. We can take the ten acres of land we have the chance of since Jamsie Dempsey died, and stock it. We will go to the fair at Ballina to buy the stock. Did Delia ask any of the money for her own use, Michael?

Michael. She did not, indeed. She did not seem to take much notice of it, or to look at it at all.

Bridget. That's no wonder. Why would she look at it when she had yourself to look at, a fine, strong young man? It is proud she must be to get you; a good steady boy that will make use of the money, and not be running through it or spending it on drink like another.

Peter. It's likely Michael himself was not thinking much of the fortune either, but of what sort the girl was to look at.

Michael [*coming over towards the table*]. Well, you would like a nice comely girl to be beside you, and to go walking with you. The fortune only lasts for a while, but the woman will be there always.

Patrick [*turning round from the window*]. They are cheering again down in the town. Maybe they are landing horses from Enniscrone. They do be cheering when the horses take the water well.

Michael. There are no horses in it. Where would they

be going and no fair at hand? Go down to the town, Patrick, and see what is going on.

Patrick [opens the door to go out, but stops for a moment on the threshold]. Will Delia remember, do you think, to bring the greyhound pup she promised me when she would be coming to the house?

Michael. She will surely.

[Patrick goes out, leaving the door open.

Peter. It will be Patrick's turn next to be looking for a fortune, but he won't find it so easy to get it and he with no place of his own.

Bridget. I do be thinking sometimes, now things are going so well with us, and the Cahels such a good back to us in the district, and Delia's own uncle a priest, we might be put in the way of making Patrick a priest some day, and he so good at his books.

Peter. Time enough, time enough. You have always your head full of plans, Bridget.

Bridget. We will be well able to give him learning, and not to send him tramping the country like a poor scholar that lives on charity.

Michael. They're not done cheering yet.

[He goes over to the door and stands there for a moment, putting up his hand to shade his eyes.

Bridget. Do you see anything?

Michael. I see an old woman coming up the path.

Bridget. Who is it, I wonder? It must be the strange woman Patrick saw a while ago.

Michael. I don't think it's one of the neighbours anyway, but she has her cloak over her face.

Bridget. It might be some poor woman heard we were making ready for the wedding and came to look for her share.

Peter. I may as well put the money out of sight. There is no use leaving it out for every stranger to look at.
    [*He goes over to a large box in the corner, opens it and puts the bag in and fumbles at the lock.*

Michael. There she is, father! [*An Old Woman passes the window slowly. She looks at Michael as she passes.*] I'd sooner a stranger not to come to the house the night before my wedding.

Bridget. Open the door, Michael; don't keep the poor woman waiting.
    [*The Old Woman comes in. Michael stands aside to make way for her.*

Old Woman. God save all here!

Peter. God save you kindly!

Old Woman. You have good shelter here.

Peter. You are welcome to whatever shelter we have.

Bridget. Sit down there by the fire and welcome.

Old Woman [*warming her hands*]. There is a hard wind outside.
    [*Michael watches her curiously from the door. Peter comes over to the table.*

Peter. Have you travelled far to-day?

Old Woman. I have travelled far, very far; there are few have travelled so far as myself, and there's many a one that doesn't make me welcome. There was one that had strong sons I thought were friends of mine, but they were shearing their sheep, and they wouldn't listen to me.

Peter. It's a pity indeed for any person to have no place of their own.

Old Woman. That's true for you indeed, and it's long I'm on the roads since I first went wandering.

Bridget. It is a wonder you are not worn out with so much wandering.

Old Woman. Sometimes my feet are tired and my hands are quiet, but there is no quiet in my heart. When the people see me quiet, they think old age has come on me and that all the stir has gone out of me. But when the trouble is on me I must be talking to my friends.

Bridget. What was it put you wandering?

Old Woman. Too many strangers in the house.

Bridget. Indeed you look as if you'd had your share of trouble.

Old Woman. I have had trouble indeed.

Bridget. What was it put the trouble on you?

Old Woman. My land that was taken from me.

Peter. Was it much land they took from you?

Old Woman. My four beautiful green fields.

Peter [aside to Bridget]. Do you think could she be the widow Casey that was put out of her holding at Kilglass a while ago?

Bridget. She is not. I saw the widow Casey one time at the market in Ballina, a stout fresh woman.

Peter [*to Old Woman*]. Did you hear a noise of cheering, and you coming up the hill?

Old Woman. I thought I heard the noise I used to hear when my friends came to visit me.
> [*She begins singing half to herself.*]
> I will go cry with the woman,
> For yellow-haired Donough is dead,
> With a hempen rope for a neckcloth,
> And a white cloth on his head,——

Michael [*coming from the door*]. What is it that you are singing, ma'am?

Old Woman. Singing I am about a man I knew one time, yellow-haired Donough that was hanged in Galway.
> [*She goes on singing, much louder.*]
> I am come to cry with you, woman,
> My hair is unwound and unbound;
> I remember him ploughing his field,
> Turning up the red side of the ground,
> And building his barn on the hill
> With the good mortared stone;
> O! we'd have pulled down the gallows
> Had it happened in Enniscrone!

Michael. What was it brought him to his death?

Old Woman. He died for love of me: many a man has died for love of me.

Peter [*aside to Bridget*]. Her trouble has put her wits astray.

Michael. Is it long since that song was made? Is it long since he got his death?

Old Woman. Not long, not long. But there were others that died for love of me a long time ago.

Michael. Were they neighbours of your own, ma'am?

Old Woman. Come here beside me and I'll tell you about them. [*Michael sits down beside her on the hearth.*] There was a red man of the O'Donells from the north, and a man of the O'Sullivans from the south, and there was one Brian that lost his life at Clontarf by the sea, and there were a great many in the west, some that died hundreds of years ago, and there are some that will die to-morrow.

Michael. Is it in the west that men will die to-morrow?

Old Woman. Come nearer, nearer to me.

Bridget. Is she right, do you think? Or is she a woman from beyond the world?

Peter. She doesn't know well what she's talking about, with the want and the trouble she has gone through.

Bridget. The poor thing, we should treat her well.

Peter. Give her a drink of milk and a bit of the oaten cake.

Bridget. Maybe we should give her something along with that, to bring her on her way. A few pence or a shilling itself, and we with so much money in the house.

Peter. Indeed I'd not begrudge it to her if we had it to spare, but if we go running through what we have, we'll soon have to break the hundred pounds, and that would be a pity.

Bridget. Shame on you, Peter. Give her the shilling and your blessing with it, or our own luck will go from us.   [*Peter goes to the box and takes out a shilling.*

Bridget [*to the Old Woman*]. Will you have a drink of milk, ma'am?

Old Woman. It is not food or drink that I want.

Peter [*offering the shilling*]. Here is something for you.

Old Woman. This is not what I want. It is not silver I want.

Peter. What is it you would be asking for?

Old Woman. If any one would give me help he must give me himself, he must give me all.

    [*Peter goes over to the table staring at the shilling in his hand in a bewildered way, and stands whispering to Bridget.*

Michael. Have you no one to care for you in your age, ma'am?

Old Woman. I have not. With all the lovers that brought me their love I never set out the bed for any.

Michael. Are you lonely going the roads, ma'am?

Old Woman. I have my thoughts and I have my hopes.

Michael. What hopes have you to hold to?

Old Woman. The hope of getting my beautiful fields back again; the hope of putting the strangers out of my house.

Michael. What way will you do that, ma'am?

Old Woman. I have good friends that will help me. They are gathering to help me now. I am not afraid. If they are put down to-day they will get the upper hand to-morrow. [*She gets up.*] I must be going to meet my friends. They are coming to help me and I must be there to welcome them. I must call the neighbours together to welcome them.

Michael. I will go with you.

Bridget. It is not her friends you have to go and welcome, Michael; it is the girl coming into the house you have to welcome. You have plenty to do; it is food and drink you have to bring to the house. The woman that is coming home is not coming with empty hands; you would not have an empty house before her. [*To the Old Woman.*] Maybe you don't know, ma'am, that my son is going to be married to-morrow.

Old Woman. It is not a man going to his marriage that I look to for help.

Peter [*to Bridget*]. Who is she, do you think, at all?

Bridget. You did not tell us your name yet, ma'am.

Old Woman. Some call me the Poor Old Woman, and there are some that call me Cathleen, the daughter of Houlihan.

Peter. I think I knew some one of that name, once. Who was it, I wonder? It must have been some one I knew when I was a boy. No, no; I remember, I heard it in a song.

Old Woman [*who is standing in the doorway*]. They are wondering that there were songs made for me; there have been many songs made for me. I heard one on the wind this morning.

[*Sings*]
Do not make a great keening
When the graves have been dug to-morrow.

>   Do not call the white-scarfed riders
>   To the burying that shall be to-morrow.
>
>   Do not spread food to call strangers
>   To the wakes that shall be to-morrow;
>   Do not give money for prayers
>   For the dead that shall die to-morrow. . . .

They will have no need of prayers, they will have no need of prayers.

Michael. I do not know what that song means, but tell me something I can do for you.

Peter. Come over to me, Michael.

Michael. Hush, father, listen to her.

Old Woman. It is a hard service they take that help me. Many that are red-cheeked now will be pale-cheeked; many that have been free to walk the hills and the bogs and the rushes will be sent to walk hard streets in far countries; many a good plan will be broken; many that have gathered money will not stay to spend it; many a child will be born and there will be no father at its christening to give it a name. They that have red cheeks will have pale cheeks for my sake, and for all that, they will think they are well paid.   [*She goes out; her voice is heard outside singing.*

>   They shall be remembered for ever,
>   They shall be alive for ever,
>   They shall be speaking for ever,
>   The people shall hear them for ever.

Bridget [*to Peter*]. Look at him, Peter; he has the look of a man that has got the touch. [*Raising her voice.*] Look here, Michael, at the wedding clothes. Such grand clothes as these are! You have a right to fit

them on now; it would be a pity to-morrow if they
did not fit. The boys would be laughing at you. Take
them, Michael, and go into the room and fit them on.
                                    [*She puts them on his arm.*

Michael. What wedding are you talking of? What clothes
will I be wearing to-morrow?

Bridget. These are the clothes you are going to wear
when you marry Delia Cahel to-morrow.

Michael. I had forgotten that.
    [*He looks at the clothes and turns towards the inner room,*
        but stops at the sound of cheering outside.

Peter. There is the shouting come to our own door.
What is it has happened?
    [*Neighbours come crowding in, Patrick and Delia with*
        them.

Patrick. There are ships in the Bay; the French are landing at Killala!
    [*Peter takes his pipe from his mouth and his hat off, and*
        stands up. The clothes slip from Michael's arm.

Delia. Michael! [*He takes no notice.*] Michael! [*He turns*
towards her.] Why do you look at me like a stranger?
        [*She drops his arm. Bridget goes over towards her.*

Patrick. The boys are all hurrying down the hillside to
join the French.

Delia. Michael won't be going to join the French.

Bridget [*to Peter*]. Tell him not to go, Peter.

Peter. It's no use. He doesn't hear a word we're saying.

Bridget. Try and coax him over to the fire.

Delia. Michael, Michael! You won't leave me! You won't join the French, and we going to be married!
  [*She puts her arms about him, he turns towards her as if about to yield.*

Old Woman's voice outside.

They shall be speaking for ever,
The people shall hear them for ever.

  [*Michael breaks away from Delia, stands for a second at the door, then rushes out, following the Old Woman's voice. Bridget takes Delia, who is crying silently, into her arms.*

Peter [*to Patrick, laying a hand on his arm*]. Did you see an old woman going down the path?

Patrick. I did not, but I saw a young girl, and she had the walk of a queen.

THE END

THE HOUR-GLASS

A Morality

(Prose Version)

1903

THE HOUR-GLASS

A Morality

PERSONS IN THE PLAY

A Wise Man   A Fool
Some Pupils   An Angel
The Wise Man's Wife and Two Children

A large room with a door at the back and another at the side opening to an inner room. A desk and a chair in the middle. An hourglass on a bracket near the door. A creepy stool near it. Some benches. An astronomical globe perhaps. Perhaps a large ancient map of the world on the wall or some musical instruments. Floor may be strewn with rushes. A Wise Man sitting at his desk.

Wise Man [*turning over the pages of a book*]. Where is that passage I am to explain to my pupils to-day? Here it is, and the book says that it was written by a beggar on the walls of Babylon: 'There are two living countries, the one visible and the one invisible; and when it is winter with us it is summer in that country, and when the November winds are up among us it is lambing-time there.' I wish that my pupils had asked me to explain any other passage. [*The Fool comes in and stands at the door holding out his hat. He has a pair of shears in the other hand.*] It sounds to me like foolishness; and yet that cannot be, for the writer of this book, where I have found so much knowledge, would not have set it by itself on this page, and surrounded it with so many images and so many deep colours and so much fine gilding, if it had been foolishness.

Fool. Give me a penny.

Wise Man [*turns to another page*]. Here he has written: 'The learned in old times forgot the visible country.' That I understand, but I have taught my learners better.

Fool. Won't you give me a penny?

Wise Man. What do you want? The words of the wise Saracen will not teach you much.

Fool. Such a great wise teacher as you are will not refuse a penny to a Fool.

Wise Man. What do you know about wisdom?

Fool. O, I know! I know what I have seen.

Wise Man. What is it you have seen?

Fool. When I went by Kilcluan, where the bells used to be ringing at the break of every day, I could hear nothing but the people snoring in their houses. When I went by Tubber-vanach, where the young men used to be climbing the hill to the blessed well, they were sitting at the cross-roads playing cards. When I went by Carrigoras, where the friars used to be fasting and serving the poor, I saw them drinking wine and obeying their wives. And when I asked what misfortune had brought all these changes, they said it was no misfortune, but it was the wisdom they had learned from your teaching.

Wise Man. Run round to the kitchen, and my wife will give you something to eat.

Fool. That is foolish advice for a wise man to give.

Wise Man. Why, Fool?

Fool. What is eaten is gone. I want pennies for my bag.

I must buy bacon in the shops, and nuts in the market, and strong drink for the time when the sun is weak. And I want snares to catch the rabbits and the squirrels and the hares, and a pot to cook them in.

Wise Man. Go away. I have other things to think of now than giving you pennies.

Fool. Give me a penny and I will bring you luck. The fishermen give me leave to sleep among the nets in their lofts in the winter-time because they say I bring them luck; and in the summer-time the wild creatures let me sleep near their nests and their holes. It is lucky even to look at me or to touch me, but it is much more lucky to give me a penny. [*Holds out his hand.*] If I wasn't lucky, I'd starve.

Wise Man. What have you got the shears for?

Fool. I won't tell you. If I told you, you would drive them away.

Wise Man. Whom would I drive away?

Fool. I won't tell you.

Wise Man. Not if I give you a penny?

Fool. No.

Wise Man. Not if I give you two pennies?

Fool. You will be very lucky if you give me two pennies, but I won't tell you!

Wise Man. Three pennies?

Fool. Four, and I will tell you!

Wise Man. Very well, four. But I will not call you Teigue the Fool any longer.

Fool. Let me come close to you where nobody will hear me. But first you must promise you will not drive them away. [*Wise Man nods.*] Every day men go out dressed in black and spread great black nets over the hills, great black nets.

Wise Man. Why do they do that?

Fool. That they may catch the feet of the angels. But every morning, just before the dawn, I go out and cut the nets with my shears, and the angels fly away.

Wise Man. Ah, now I know that you are Teigue the Fool. You have told me that I am wise, and I have never seen an angel.

Fool. I have seen plenty of angels.

Wise Man. Do you bring luck to the angels too?

Fool. O, no, no! No one could do that. But they are always there if one looks about one; they are like the blades of grass.

Wise Man. When do you see them?

Fool. When one gets quiet, then something wakes up inside one, something happy and quiet like the stars —not like the seven that move, but like the fixed stars.

Wise Man. And what happens then?

Fool. Then all in a minute one smells summer flowers, and tall people go by, happy and laughing, and their clothes are the colour of burning sods.

Wise Man. Is it long since you have seen them, Teigue the Fool?

Fool. Not long, glory be to God! I saw one coming behind me just now. It was not laughing, but it had clothes the colour of burning sods, and there was something shining about its head.

Wise Man. Well, there are your four pennies. You, a Fool, say 'Glory be to God', but before I came the wise men said it. Run away now. I must ring the bell for my scholars.

Fool. Four pennies! That means a great deal of luck. Great teacher, I have brought you plenty of luck!

[*He goes out shaking the bag.*

Wise Man. Though they call him Teigue the Fool, he is not more foolish than everybody used to be, with their dreams and their preachings and their three worlds; but I have overthrown their three worlds with the seven sciences. [*He touches the books with his hands.*] With Philosophy that was made from the lonely star, I have taught them to forget Theology; with Architecture, I have hidden the ramparts of their cloudy Heaven; with Music, the fierce planets' daughter whose hair is always on fire, and with Grammar that is the moon's daughter, I have shut their ears to the imaginary harpings and speech of the angels; and I have made formations of battle with Arithmetic that have put the hosts of Heaven to the rout. But, Rhetoric and Dialectic, that have been born out of the light star and out of the amorous star, you have been my spearman and my catapult! O! my swift horsemen! O! my keen darting arguments, it is because of you that I have overthrown the hosts of foolishness! [*An Angel, in a dress the colour of embers, and carrying a blossoming apple bough in her hand and a gilded halo about her head, stands upon the threshold.*] Before I came, men's minds were stuffed with folly about a Heaven where birds sang the hours, and about angels that came and stood upon men's thresholds. But I have locked the visions into Heaven and turned the key upon them. Well, I must consider this passage about the two countries. My mother used to say something of the kind. She would say that when our bodies sleep our souls awake, and that whatever withers here ripens yonder, and that harvests are snatched from us that they may feed invisible people. But the meaning of the book may be different, for only fools and women have thoughts like that; their thoughts were never written upon the walls of Babylon. [*He sees the Angel.*] What are you? Who are you? I think I saw some that were like you in my dreams when I was a child—that bright thing, that dress that is the colour of embers! But I have done with dreams, I have done with dreams.

Angel. I am the Angel of the Most High God.

Wise Man. Why have you come to me?

Angel. I have brought you a message.

Wise Man. What message have you got for me?

Angel. You will die within the hour. You will die when the last grains have fallen in this glass. [*She turns the hour-glass.*]

Wise Man. My time to die has not come. I have my pupils. I have a young wife and children that I cannot leave. Why must I die?

Angel. You must die because no souls have passed over the threshold of Heaven since you came into this country. The threshold is grassy, and the gates are rusty, and the angels that keep watch there are lonely.

Wise Man. Where will death bring me to?

Angel. The doors of Heaven will not open to you, for you have denied the existence of Heaven; and the doors of Purgatory will not open to you, for you have denied the existence of Purgatory.

Wise Man. But I have also denied the existence of Hell!

Angel. Hell is the place of those who deny.

Wise Man [*kneels*]. I have, indeed, denied everything, and have taught others to deny. I have believed in nothing but what my senses told me. But, O! beautiful angel, forgive me, forgive me!

Angel. You should have asked forgiveness long ago.

Wise Man. Had I seen your face as I see it now, O! beautiful angel, I would have believed, I would have asked forgiveness. Maybe you do not know how easy it is to doubt. Storm, death, the grass rotting, many sicknesses, those are the messengers that came to me. O! why are you silent? You carry the pardon of the Most High; give it to me! I would kiss your hands if I were not afraid—no, no, the hem of your dress!

Angel. You let go undying hands too long ago to take hold of them now.

Wise Man. You cannot understand. You live in a country that we can only dream about. Maybe it is as hard for you to understand why we disbelieve as it is for us to believe. O! what have I said? You know everything! Give me time to undo what I have done. Give me a year—a month—a day—an hour! Give me to this hour's end, that I may undo what I have done!

Angel. You cannot undo what you have done. Yet I have this power with my message. If you can find one that believes before the hour's end, you shall come to Heaven after the years of Purgatory. For, from one fiery seed, watched over by those that sent me, the harvest can come again to heap the golden threshing-floor. But now farewell, for I am weary with the weight of time.

Wise Man. Blessed be the Father, blessed be the Son, blessed be the Spirit, blessed be the Messenger They have sent!

Angel [*at the door, and pointing at the hour-glass*]. In a little while the uppermost glass will be empty.

[*Goes out.*

Wise Man. Everything will be well with me. I will call my pupils; they only say they doubt. [*Pulls the bell.*] They will be here in a moment. I hear their feet outside on the path. They want to please me; they pretend that they disbelieve. Belief is too old to be overcome all in a minute. Besides I can prove what I once disproved. [*Another pull at the bell.*] They are coming now. I will go to my desk. I will speak quietly, as if nothing had happened.

[*He stands at the desk with a fixed look in his eyes.*

Enter Pupils and the Fool

Fool. Leave me alone. Leave me alone. Who is that pulling at my bag? King's son, do not pull at my bag.

A Young Man. Did your friends the angels give you that bag? Why don't they fill your bag for you?

Fool. Give me pennies! Give me some pennies!

A Young Man. What do you want pennies for? That great bag at your waist is heavy.

Fool. I want to buy bacon in the shops, and nuts in the market, and strong drink for the time when the sun is weak, and snares to catch rabbits and the squirrels that steal the nuts, and hares, and a great pot to cook them in.

A Young Man. Why don't your friends tell you where buried treasures are?

Another. Why don't they make you dream about treasures? If one dreams three times there is always treasure.

Fool [*holding out his hat*]. Give me pennies! Give me pennies!
> [*They throw pennies into his hat. He is standing close to the door, that he may hold out his hat to each newcomer.*

A Young Man. Master, will you have Teigue the Fool for a scholar?

Another Young Man. Teigue, will you give us your pennies if we teach you lessons? No, he goes to school for nothing on the mountains. Tell us what you learn on the mountains, Teigue?

Wise Man. Be silent all! [*He has been standing silent, looking away.*] Stand still in your places, for there is something I would have you tell me.
> [*A moment's pause. They all stand round in their places. Teigue still stands at the door.*

Wise Man. Is there any one amongst you who believes in God? In Heaven? Or in Purgatory? Or in Hell?

All the Young Men. No one, Master! No one!

Wise Man. I knew you would all say that; but do not be afraid. I will not be angry. Tell me the truth. Do you not believe?

A Young Man. We once did, but you have taught us to know better.

Wise Man. O! teaching, teaching does not go very deep! The heart remains unchanged under it all. You have the faith that you always had, and you are afraid to tell me.

A Young Man. No, no, Master!

Wise Man. If you tell me that you have not changed, I shall be glad and not angry.

A Young Man [*to his Neighbour*]. He wants somebody to dispute with.

His Neighbour. I knew that from the beginning.

A Young Man. That is not the subject for to-day; you were going to talk about the words the beggar wrote upon the walls of Babylon.

Wise Man. If there is one amongst you that has not changed, he will be my best friend. Surely there is one amongst you. [*They are all silent.*] Surely what you learned at your mothers' knees has not been so soon forgotten.

A Young Man. Master, till you came, no teacher in this land was able to get rid of foolishness and ignorance. But every one has listened to you, every one has learned the truth. You have had your last disputation.

Another. What a fool you made of that monk in the market-place! He had not a word to say.

Wise Man [*comes from his desk and stands among them in the middle of the room*]. Pupils, dear friends, I have deceived you all this time. It was I myself who was ignorant. There is a God. There is a Heaven. There is fire that passes and there is fire that lasts for ever.

[*Teigue, through all this, is sitting on a stool by the door, reckoning on his fingers what he will buy with his money.*

A Young Man [*to another*]. He will not be satisfied till we dispute with him. [*To the Wise Man*] Prove it, Master. Have you seen them?

Wise Man [*in a low, solemn voice*]. Just now, before you came in, some one came to the door, and when I looked up I saw an angel standing there.

A Young Man. You were in a dream. Anybody can see an angel in his dreams.

Wise Man. O, my God! It was not a dream! I was awake, waking as I am now. I tell you I was awake as I am now.

A Young Man. Some dream when they are awake, but they are the crazy, and who would believe what they say? Forgive me, Master, but that is what you taught me to say. That is what you said to the monk when he spoke of the visions of the saints and the martyrs.

Another Young Man. You see how well we remember your teaching.

Wise Man. Out, out from my sight! I want somebody who has not changed. That is the grain the angel spoke of—I must find it before I die. I tell you I must find it. The sands are falling there and you answer me with arguments. Out with you, out of my sight!   [*The Young Men laugh.*

A Young Man. How well he plays at faith! He is like the monk when he had nothing more to say.

Wise Man. Out, out, this is no time for laughter! Out with you, though you are a king's son!

[*They begin to hurry out.*

A Young Man. Come, come; he wants us to find some one who will dispute with him.   [*All go out.*

Wise Man [*alone; he goes to the door at the side*]. I will call my wife. She will believe; women always believe. [*He opens the door and calls.*] Bridget! Bridget! [*Bridget comes in wearing her apron, her sleeves turned up from her floury arms.*] Bridget, tell me the truth; do not say what you think will please me. Do you sometimes say your prayers?

Bridget. Prayers! No, you taught me to leave them off long ago. At first I was sorry, but I am glad now, for I am sleepy in the evenings.

Wise Man. But do you not believe in God?

Bridget. O, a good wife only believes what her husband tells her!

Wise Man. But sometimes when you are alone, when I am in the school and the children asleep, do you not think about the saints, about the things you used to believe in? What do you think of when you are alone?

Bridget [*considering*]. I think about nothing. Sometimes

I wonder if the linen is bleaching white, or I go out to see if the crows are picking up the chickens' food.

Wise Man. O, what can I do! Is there nobody who believes he can never die? I must go and find somebody! [*He goes towards the door, but stops with his eyes fixed on the hour-glass.*] I cannot go out; I cannot leave that. Go and call my pupils again. I will make them understand. I will say to them that only amid spiritual terror or only when all that laid hold on life is shaken can we see truth. There is something in Plato, but —No, do not call them. They would answer as I have bid.

Bridget. You want somebody to get up an argument with.

Wise Man. O, look out of the door and tell me if there is anybody there in the street. I cannot leave this glass; somebody might shake it! Then the sand would fall more quickly.

Bridget. I don't understand what you are saying. [*Looks out.*] There is a great crowd of people talking to your pupils.

Wise Man. O, run out, Bridget, and see if they have found somebody that, all the time I was teaching, understood nothing or did not listen!

Bridget [*wiping her arms in her apron and pulling down her sleeves*]. It's a hard thing to be married to a man of learning that must be always having arguments. [*Goes out and shouts through the kitchen door.*] Don't be meddling with the bread, children, while I'm out.

Wise Man [*kneels down*]. 'Confiteor Deo Omnipotenti, beatae Mariae—salvum—salvum . . .' I have forgotten it all.

It is thirty years since I have said a prayer. I must pray in the common tongue, like the clown begging in the market, like Teigue the Fool! [*He prays.*] Help me, Father, Son and Spirit!

[*Bridget enters, followed by the Fool, who is holding out his hat to her.*]

Fool. Give me something; give me a penny to buy bacon in the shops, and nuts in the market, and strong drink for the time when the sun grows weak.

Bridget. I have no pennies. [*To the Wise Man.*] Your pupils cannot find anybody to argue with you. There is nobody in the whole country who has enough belief to fill a pipe since you put down the monk. Can't you be quiet now and not always wanting to have arguments? It must be terrible to have a mind like that.

Wise Man. I am lost! I am lost!

Bridget. Leave me alone now; I have to make the bread for you and the children.

Wise Man. Out of this, woman, out of this, I say! [*Bridget goes through the kitchen door.*] Will nobody find a way to help me! But she spoke of my children. I had forgotten them. They will not have changed. It is only those who have reason that doubt; the young are full of faith. Bridget, Bridget, send my children to me.

Bridget [*inside*]. Your father wants you; run to him now.

[*The two Children come in. They stand together a little way from the threshold of the kitchen door, looking timidly at their father.*]

Wise Man. Children, what do you believe? Is there a Heaven? Is there a Hell? Is there a Purgatory?

First Child. We haven't forgotten, father.

The Other Child. O no, father. [*They both speak together as if in school.*] There is nothing we cannot see; there is nothing we cannot touch.

First Child. Foolish people used to think that there was, but you are very learned and you have taught us better.

Wise Man. You are just as bad as the others, just as bad as the others! Do not run away! Come back to me! [*The Children begin to cry and run away.*] Why are you afraid? I will teach you better—no, I will never teach you again. Go to your mother! no, she will not be able to teach them . . . Help them, O God! . . . The grains are going very quickly. There is very little sand in the uppermost glass. Somebody will come for me in a moment; perhaps he is at the door now! All creatures that have reason doubt. O that the grass and the plants could speak! Somebody has said that they would wither if they doubted. O, speak to me, O grass-blades! O fingers of God's certainty, speak to me! You are millions and you will not speak. I dare not know the moment the messenger will come for me. I will cover the glass. [*He covers it with a cloth. Sees the Fool, who is sitting by the door playing with some flowers which he has stuck in his hat. He has begun to blow a dandelion head.*] What are you doing?

Fool. Wait a moment. [*He blows.*] Four, five, six.

Wise Man. What are you doing that for?

Fool. I am blowing at the dandelion to find out what time it is.

Wise Man. You have heard everything! That is why you want to find out what hour it is! You are waiting to see them coming through the door to carry me away. [*Fool goes on blowing.*] I will not have you sitting there. I will have no one here when they come. [*He seizes the Fool by the shoulders, and begins to force him out through the door, then suddenly changes his mind.*] No, I have something to ask you. [*He drags him back into the room.*] Is there a Heaven? Is there a Hell? Is there a Purgatory?

Fool. So you ask me now. I thought when you were asking your pupils, I said to myself, if he would ask Teigue the Fool, Teigue could tell him all about it, for Teigue has learned all about it when he has been cutting the nets.

Wise Man. Tell me quickly!

Fool. I said, Teigue knows everything. Not even the cats or the hares that milk the cows have Teigue's wisdom. But Teigue will not speak; he says nothing.

Wise Man. Tell me, tell me! For under the cover the grains are falling, and when they are all fallen I shall die; and my soul will be lost if I have not found somebody that knows and believes! Speak, speak!

Fool [*looking wise*]. I will not speak! I will not tell you what is in my mind, and I won't tell you what is in my bag. You might steal away my thoughts. I met a bodach on the road yesterday, and he said, 'Teigue, tell me how many pennies are in your bag; I will wager three pennies that there are not twenty pennies

in your bag; let me put in my hand and count them.'
But I pulled the strings tighter, like this; and when
I go to sleep every night I hide the bag where no one
knows.

Wise Man [*goes towards the hour-glass as if to uncover it*]. No,
no, I have not the courage. [*He kneels.*] Have pity upon
me, Fool, and tell me!

Fool. Ah, now that is different. I am not afraid of you
now. What is that I am to tell you? But I must come
near; somebody in there might hear what the angel
said.

Wise Man. But speak and I am saved. What did the
angel say to you?

Fool. O no, no, no. How could poor Teigue see angels?
O, Teigue tells one tale here, another tale there,
and everybody gives him pennies. If Teigue had not
his tales he would starve.

                       [*He backs away and goes out.*

Wise Man. My last hope is gone and now that it is too
late I can see it all. Those words about winter and
summer, about our November being the lambing-
time in that other country—all, all is plain now. We
sink in on God, we find Him in becoming nothing
—we perish into reality.   [*The Fool comes back.*

Fool. There was one there—there by the threshold stone,
writing there; and she said, 'Go in, Teigue, and tell
him everything that he asks you. He will give you a
penny if you tell him.'

Wise Man. We perish into reality—strange that I never
saw it until now.

Fool. Will you give me a penny if I tell you?

Wise Man. O no, do not tell me anything. I am content to know that God's will prevails whatever that be.

Fool. Waiting till the moment had come—that is what the one out there was saying, but I might tell you what you asked. That is what he was saying.

Wise Man. Be silent. May God's will prevail though that be my damnation! What was I born for but that I might cry that His will be fulfilled upon the instant, though that be my damnation? I am dying. The sand has run out. Ring the bell, ring for my pupils. [*Fool rings.*] For I am going from the country of the seven wandering stars, and am going to the country of the fixed stars. [*Voices of Pupils singing.*] They are coming. I must make all plain to them, that they may wish His will be fulfilled though that be our damnation. There is no other truth.   [*Dies.*

Pupils enter

Young Man. Look at the Fool turned bell-ringer.

Another. What have you called us in for, Teigue?

Fool. There was something he wanted to say, but you must wake him, he has fallen asleep.

Young Man. No wonder he has dreams. He is so fast asleep that I cannot wake him. O, he is dead. . . .

Pupils gather round

Fool. Look, look, what has come from his mouth . . . a little winged thing . . . a little shining thing . . . it has gone to the door. . . . O, look, there in the door.... [*The Angel appears at the door, she opens her hands and closes them again.*] The Angel has taken it in her hands.

A Young Man. What are you pointing at?

Fool. The Angel has taken it in her hands. She will open her hands in the Garden of Paradise.

Young Man. There is nobody there—there is nobody in the door.

THE END

THE POT OF BROTH

1904

THE POT OF BROTH

PERSONS IN THE PLAY

John Coneely, *an elderly man*
Sibby Coneely, *a young or middle-aged woman*
A Tramp

A cottage kitchen. Fire on the hearth; table with cabbage, onions, a plate of meal, etc. Half-open door. A Tramp enters, looks about.

Tramp. What sort are the people of this house, I wonder? Was it a good place for me to come to look for my dinner, I wonder? What's in that big pot? [*Lifts cover.*] Nothing at all! What's in the little pot? [*Lifts cover.*] Nothing at all! What's in that bottle, I wonder? [*Takes it up excitedly and tastes.*] Milk! milk in a bottle! I wonder they wouldn't afford a tin can to milk the cow into! Not much chance for a poor man to make a living here. What's in that chest? [*Kneels and tries to lift cover.*] Locked! [*Smells at the key-hole.*] There's a good smell—there must be a still not far off.

[*Gets up and sits on chest. A noise heard outside, shouts, footsteps, and loud frightened cackling.*

Tramp. What in the earthly world is going on outside? Any one would think it was the Fiannta-h-Eireann at their hunting!

Sibby's voice. Stop the gap, let you stop the gap, John.

Stop that old schemer of a hen flying up on the thatch like as if she was an eagle!

John's voice. What can I do, Sibby? I all to had my hand upon her when she flew away!

Sibby's voice. She's out into the garden! Follow after her! She has the wide world before her now.

Tramp. Sibby he called her. I wonder is it Sibby Coneely's house I am in? If that's so it's a bad chance I have of going out heavier than I came in. I often heard of her, a regular slave-driver that would starve the rats. A niggard with her eyes on kippeens, that would skin a flea for its hide! It was the bad luck of the world brought me here, and not a house or a village between this and Tubber. And it isn't much I have left to bring me on there. [*Begins emptying out his pockets on the chest.*] There's my pipe and not a grain to fill it with! There's my handkerchief I got at the coronation dinner! There's my knife and nothing left of it but the handle. [*Shakes his pocket out.*] And there's a crust of the last dinner I got, and the last I'm likely to get till to-morrow. That's all I have in the world unless the stone I picked up to pelt at that yelping dog a while ago. [*Takes stone out of pocket and tosses it up and down.*] In the time long ago I usen't to have much trouble to find a dinner, getting over the old women and getting round the young ones! I remember the time I met the old minister on the path and sold him his own flock of turkeys. My wits used to fill my stomach then, but I'm afraid they're going from me now with all the hardship I went through. [*Cackling heard again and cries.*

Sibby's voice. Catch her, she's round the bush! Put your hands in the nettles, don't be daunted!

> [*A choked cackle and prolonged screech.*

Tramp. There's a dinner for somebody anyway. That it may be for myself! How will I come round her, I wonder? There is no more pity in her heart than there's a soul in a dog. If all the saints were standing barefoot before her she'd bid them to call another day. It's myself I have to trust to now, and my share of talk. [*Looks at the stone.*] I know what I'll do, I know what the tinker did with a stone, and I'm as good a man as he is anyway. [*He jumps up and waves the stone over his head.*] Now, Sibby! If I don't do it one way I'll do it another. My wits against the world!

> There's broth in the pot for you, old man,
> There's broth in the pot for you, old man,
>> There's cabbage for me
>> And broth for you,
> And beef for Jack the journeyman.
>
> I wish you were dead, my gay old man,
> I wish you were dead, my gay old man,
> I wish you were dead
> And a stone at your head,
> So as I'd marry poor Jack the journeyman.

John's voice [*outside*]. Bring it in, bring it in, Sibby. You'll be late with the priest's dinner.

Sibby's voice. Can't you wait a minute till I'll draw it?

Enter John

John. I didn't know there was any one in the house.

Tramp. It's only this minute I came in, tired with the length of the road I am, and fasting since morning.

John [*begins groping among the pots and pans*]. I'll see can I find anything here for you . . . I don't see much . . . Maybe there's something in the chest.

> [*He takes key from a hiding-place at back of hearth, opens chest, takes out bottle, takes out a ham-bone and is cutting a bit from it when Sibby enters, carrying chicken by the neck. John drops the ham-bone on a bench.*

Sibby. Hurry now, John, after all the time you have wasted. Why didn't you steal up on the old hen that time she was scratching in the dust?

John. Sure I thought one of the chickens would be the tenderest.

Sibby. Cock you up with tenderness! All the expense I'm put to! My grand hen I've been feeding these five years! Wouldn't that have been enough to part with? Indeed I wouldn't have thought of parting with her itself, but she had got tired of laying since Easter.

John. Well, I thought we ought to give his Reverence something that would have a little good in it.

Sibby. What does the age of it matter? A hen's a hen when it's on the table. [*Sitting down to pluck chicken.*] Why couldn't the Kernans have given the priest his dinner the way they always do? What did it matter their mother's brother to have died? It is an excuse they had made up to put the expense of the dinner on me.

John. Well, I hope you have a good bit of bacon to put in the pot along with the chicken.

Sibby. Let me alone. The taste of meat on the knife is all that high-up people like the clergy care for, nice genteel people, no way greedy like potato-diggers or harvest men.

John. Well, I never saw the man, gentle or simple, wouldn't be glad of his fill of bacon and he hungry.

Sibby. Let me alone, I'll show the Kernans what I can do. I have what is better than bacon, a nice bit of a ham I am keeping in the chest this good while, thinking we might want it for company. [*She catches sight of Tramp and calls out.*] Who is there? A beggar-man, is it? Then you may quit this house if you please. We have nothing for you. [*She gets up and opens the door.*]

Tramp [*comes forward*]. It is a mistake you are making, ma'am, it is not asking anything I am. It is giving I am more used to. I was never in a house yet but there would be a welcome for me in it again.

Sibby. Well, you have the appearance of a beggar, and if it isn't begging you are, what way do you make your living?

Tramp. If I was a beggar, ma'am, it is to common people I would be going and not to a nice grand woman like yourself, that is only used to be talking with high-up noble people.

Sibby. Well, what is it you are asking? If it's a bit to eat you want, I can't give it to you, for I have company coming that will clear all before them.

Tramp. Is it me ask anything to eat? [*Holds up stone.*] I have here what is better than beef and mutton, and currant cakes and sacks of flour.

Sibby. What is it at all?

Tramp [*mysteriously*]. Those that gave it to me wouldn't like me to tell that.

Sibby [*to John*]. Do you think is he a man that has friends among the Sidhe?

John. Your mind is always running on the Sidhe since the time they made John Molloy find buried gold on the bridge of Limerick. I see nothing in it but a stone.

Tramp. What can you see in it, you that never saw what it can do?

John. What is it it can do?

Tramp. It can do many things, and what it's going to do now is to make me a drop of broth for my dinner.

Sibby. I'd like to have a stone that could make broth.

Tramp. No one in the world but myself has one, ma'am, and no other stone in the world has the same power, for it has enchantment on it. All I'll ask of you now, ma'am, is the loan of a pot with a drop of boiling water in it.

Sibby. You're welcome to that much. John, fill the small pot with water. [*John fills the pot from a kettle.*

Tramp [*putting in stone*]. There now, that's all I have to do but to put it on the fire to boil, and it's a grand pot of broth will be before me then.

Sibby. And is that all you have to put in it?

Tramp. Nothing at all but that—only, maybe, a bit of an herb for fear the enchantment might slip away from it. You wouldn't have a bit of Slanlus in the house, ma'am, that was cut with a black-handled knife?

Sibby. No, indeed, I have none of that in the house.

Tramp. Or a bit of the Fearavan that was picked when the wind was from the north?

Sibby. No, indeed, I'm sorry there's none.

Tramp. Or a sprig of the Athair-talav, the father of herbs?

John. There's plenty of it by the hedge. I'll go out and get it for you.

Tramp. O, don't mind taking so much trouble; those leaves beside me will do well enough. [*He takes a couple of good handfuls of the cabbage and onions and puts them in.*]

Sibby. But where at all did you get the stone?

Tramp. Well, this is how it happened. I was out one time, and a grand greyhound with me, and it followed a hare, and I went after it. And I came up at last to the edge of a gravel pit where there were a few withered furze bushes, and there was my fine hound sitting up, and it shivering, and a little old man sitting before it, and he taking off a hareskin coat. [*Looking round at the ham-bone.*] Give me the loan of a kippeen to stir the pot with. . . . [*He takes the ham-bone and puts it into the pot.*]

John. Oh! the ham-bone!

Tramp. I didn't say a ham-bone, I said a hareskin coat.

Sibby. Hold your tongue, John, if it's deaf you are getting.

Tramp [*stirring the pot with the ham-bone*]. Well, as I was telling you, he was sitting up, and one time I thought

he was as small as a nut, and the next minute I
thought his head to be in the stars. Frightened I was.

Sibby. No wonder, no wonder at all in that.

Tramp. He took the little stone then—that stone I have
with me—out of the side pocket of his coat, and he
showed it to me. 'Call off your dog', says he, 'and
I'll give you that stone, and if ever you want a good
drop of broth or a bit of stirabout, or a drop of poteen
itself, all you have to do is to put it down in a pot
with a drop of water and stir it awhile, and you'll
have the thing you were wanting ready before you.'

Sibby. Poteen! Would it make that?

Tramp. It would, ma'am; and wine, the same as the
Clare Militia uses.

Sibby. Let me see what does it look like now. [*Is bending forward.*]

Tramp. Don't look at it for your life, ma'am. It might
bring bad luck on any one that would look at it, and
it boiling. I must put a cover on the pot, or I must
colour the water some way. Give me a handful of
that meal.

[*Sibby holds out a plate of meal and he puts in a handful
or two.*

John. Well, he is a gifted man!

Sibby. It would be a great comfort to have a stone like
that. [*She has finished plucking the chicken which lies in
her lap.*]

Tramp. And there's another thing it does, ma'am, since
it came into Catholic hands. If you put it into a pot
of a Friday with a bit of the whitest meat in Ireland
in it, it would turn it as black as black.

Sibby. That is no less than a miracle. I must tell Father John about that.

Tramp. But to put a bit of meat with it any other day of the week, it would do it no harm at all, but good. Look here now, ma'am, I'll put that nice little hen you have in your lap in the pot for a minute till you'll see. [*Takes it and puts it in.*]

John [*sarcastically*]. It's a good job this is not a Friday!

Sibby. Keep yourself quiet, John, and don't be interrupting the talk or you'll get a knock on the head like the King of Lochlann's grandmother.

John. Go on, go on, I'll say no more.

Tramp. If I'm passing this way some time of a Friday, I'll bring a nice bit of mutton, or the breast of a turkey, and you'll see how it will be no better in two minutes than a fistful of bog mould.

Sibby [*getting up*]. Let me take the chicken out now.

Tramp. Stop till I'll help you, ma'am, you might scald your hand. I'll show it to you in a minute as white as your own skin, where the lily and the rose are fighting for mastery. Did you ever hear what the boys in your own parish were singing after you being married from them—such of them that had any voice at all and not choked with crying, or senseless with the drop of drink they took to comfort them and to keep their wits from going, with the loss of you?
[*Sibby sits down again complacently.*

Sibby. Did they do that indeed?

Tramp. They did, ma'am, this is what they used to be singing:

> Philomel, I've listened oft
> To thy lay, near weeping willow—

No, that's not it—it's a queer thing the memory is—

> 'Twas at the dance at Dermody's that first I
> caught a sight of her.

No, that's not it either—ah, now I have it.

> My pretty Paistin is my heart's desire,
> Yet am I shrunken to skin and bone.

Sibby. Why would they call me Paistin?

Tramp. And why wouldn't they? Would you wish them to put your right name in a song, and your man ready to knock the brains of any man will as much as look your side of the road?

Sibby. Well, maybe so.

Tramp. I was standing by the man that made the song, and he writing it with an old bit of a carpenter's pencil, and the tears running down—

> My pretty Paistin is my heart's desire,
> Yet am I shrunken to skin and bone,
> For all that my heart has had for its hire
> Is what I can whistle alone and alone.
>   *Aro, Aro.*
> *Tomorrow night I will break down the door.*

[*Sibby takes a fork and rises to take out the chicken. Tramp puts his hand to stop her and goes on:*

> What is the good of a man and he

Alone and alone with a speckled shin?
I would that I drank with my love on my knee,
Between two barrels at the inn.
    Aro, Aro.
Tomorrow night I will break down the door.

  [*Sibby half rises again. Tramp puts his hand upon her hand.*

Tramp. Wait now till you hear the end [*sings*]:

Alone and alone nine nights I lay
Between two bushes under the rain;
I thought to have whistled her down that way,
I whistled and whistled and whistled in vain.
    Aro, Aro.
Tomorrow night I will break down the door.

  [*He repeats the verse, Sibby singing too and beating time with fork.*

Sibby [*to John*]. I always knew I was too good for you! [*She goes on humming.*]

John. Well, he has the poor woman bewitched.

Sibby [*suddenly coming to her wits*]. Did you take the chicken out yet?

Tramp [*taking it out and giving it a good squeeze into the pot*]. I did, ma'am. Look at it there.

                  [*He takes it and lays it on table.*

John. How is the broth getting on?

Tramp [*tasting it with a spoon*]. It's grand. It's always grand.

Sibby. Give me a taste of it.

Tramp [*takes the pot off and slips the ham-bone behind him*].

Give me some vessel till I'll give this sky-woman a taste of it.

> [*John gives him an egg-cup which he fills and gives to Sibby. John gives him a mug, and he fills this for himself, pouring it back and forward from the mug to a bowl that is on the table, and drinking gulps now and again. Sibby blows at hers and smells it.*]

Sibby. There's a good smell on it anyway. [*Tasting.*] It's lovely. O, I'd give the world and all to have the stone that made that!

Tramp. The world and all wouldn't buy it, ma'am. If I was inclined to sell it the Lord Lieutenant would have given me Dublin Castle and all that's in it long ago.

Sibby. O, couldn't we coax it out of you any way at all?

Tramp [*drinking more soup*]. The whole world wouldn't coax it out of me except maybe for one thing . . . [*looks depressed*]. Now I think of it, there's only one reason I might think of parting with it at all.

Sibby [*eagerly*]. What reason is that?

Tramp. It's a misfortune that overtakes me, ma'am, every time I make an attempt to keep a pot of my own to boil it in, and I don't like to be always under a compliment to the neighbours, asking the loan of one. But whatever way it is, I never can keep a pot with me. I had a right to ask one of the little man that gave me the stone. The last one I bought got the bottom burned out of it one night I was giving a hand to a friend that keeps a still, and the one before that I hid under a bush one time I was going into Ennis for the night, and some boys in the town dreamed about it and went looking for treasure in it, and they found nothing but eggshells, but they brought it away for all that. And another one . . .

Sibby. Give me the loan of the stone itself, and I'll engage I'll keep a pot for it. . . . Wait now till I'll make some offer to you. . . .

Tramp [*aside*]. I'd best not be stopping to bargain, the priest might be coming in on me. [*Gets up.*] Well, ma'am, I'm sorry I can't oblige you. [*Goes to door, shades his eyes and looks out, turns suddenly.*] I have no time to lose, ma'am, I'm off. [*Comes to table and takes his hat.*] Well, ma'am, what offer will you make?

John. You might as well leave it for a day on trial first.

Tramp [*to John*]. I think it likely I'll not be passing this way again. [*To Sibby.*] Well, now, ma'am, as you were so kind, and for the sake of the good treatment you gave me, I'll ask nothing at all for it. Here it is for you and welcome, and that you may live long to use it! But I'll just take a little bit in my bag that'll do for my supper, for fear I mightn't be in Tubber before night. [*He takes up the chicken.*] And you won't begrudge me a drop of whisky when you can make plenty for yourself from this out. [*Takes the bottle.*]

John. You deserve it, you deserve it indeed. You are a very gifted man. Don't forget the kippeen!

Tramp. It's here! [*Slaps his pocket and exit. John follows him.*]

Sibby [*looking at the stone in her hand*]. Broth of the best, stirabout, poteen, wine itself, he said! And the people

F

that will be coming to see the miracle! I'll be as rich as Biddy Early before I die!   [*John comes back.*

Sibby. Where were you, John?

John. I just went out to shake him by the hand. He's a very gifted man.

Sibby. He is so indeed.

John. And the priest's at the top of the boreen coming for his dinner. Maybe you'd best put the stone in the pot again.

THE END

ON BAILE'S STRAND

1904

ON BAILE'S STRAND

PERSONS IN THE PLAY

A Fool
A Blind Man
Cuchulain, *King of Muirthemne*
Conchubar, *High King of Ulad*
A Young Man, *son of Cuchulain*
Kings and Singing Women

A great hall at Dundealgan, not 'Cuchulain's great ancient house' but an assembly house nearer to the sea. A big door at the back, and through the door misty light as of sea-mist. There are many chairs and one long bench. One of these chairs, which is towards the front of the stage, is bigger than the others. Somewhere at the back there is a table with flagons of ale upon it and drinking-horns. There is a small door at one side of the hall. A Fool and Blind Man, both ragged, and their features made grotesque and extravagant by masks, come in through the door at the back. The Blind Man leans upon a staff.

Fool. What a clever man you are though you are blind! There's nobody with two eyes in his head that is as clever as you are. Who but you could have thought that the henwife sleeps every day a little at noon? I would never be able to steal anything if you didn't tell me where to look for it. And what a good cook you are! You take the fowl out of my hands after I have stolen it and plucked it, and you put it into

the big pot at the fire there, and I can go out and run
races with the witches at the edge of the waves and
get an appetite, and when I've got it, there's the hen
waiting inside for me, done to the turn.

Blind Man [*who is feeling about with his stick*]. Done to the
turn.

Fool [*putting his arm round Blind Man's neck*]. Come now,
I'll have a leg and you'll have a leg, and we'll draw
lots for the wish-bone. I'll be praising you, I'll be
praising you while we're eating it, for your good
plans and for your good cooking. There's nobody in
the world like you, Blind Man. Come, come. Wait a
minute. I shouldn't have closed the door. There are
some that look for me, and I wouldn't like them not
to find me. Don't tell it to anybody, Blind Man.
There are some that follow me. Boann herself out
of the river and Fand out of the deep sea. Witches
they are, and they come by in the wind, and they
cry, 'Give a kiss, Fool, give a kiss', that's what they
cry. That's wide enough. All the witches can come
in now. I wouldn't have them beat at the door and
say, 'Where is the Fool? Why has he put a lock on
the door?' Maybe they'll hear the bubbling of the
pot and come in and sit on the ground. But we won't
give them any of the fowl. Let them go back to the
sea, let them go back to the sea.

Blind Man [*feeling legs of big chair with his hands*]. Ah!
[*Then, in a louder voice as he feels the back of it.*] Ah—
ah—

Fool. Why do you say 'Ah-ah'?

Blind Man. I know the big chair. It is to-day the High
King Conchubar is coming. They have brought out

his chair. He is going to be Cuchulain's master in earnest from this day out. It is that he's coming for.

Fool. He must be a great man to be Cuchulain's master.

Blind Man. So he is. He is a great man. He is over all the rest of the kings of Ireland.

Fool. Cuchulain's master! I thought Cuchulain could do anything he liked.

Blind Man. So he did, so he did. But he ran too wild, and Conchubar is coming to-day to put an oath upon him that will stop his rambling and make him as biddable as a house-dog and keep him always at his hand. He will sit in this chair and put the oath upon him.

Fool. How will he do that?

Blind Man. You have no wits to understand such things. [*The Blind Man has got into the chair.*] He will sit up in this chair and he'll say: 'Take the oath, Cuchulain. I bid you take the oath. Do as I tell you. What are your wits compared with mine, and what are your riches compared with mine? And what sons have you to pay your debts and to put a stone over you when you die? Take the oath, I tell you. Take a strong oath.'

Fool [*crumpling himself up and whining*]. I will not. I'll take no oath. I want my dinner.

Blind Man. Hush, hush! It is not done yet.

Fool. You said it was done to a turn.

Blind Man. Did I, now? Well, it might be done, and not done. The wings might be white, but the legs

might be red. The flesh might stick hard to the
bones and not come away in the teeth. But, believe
me, Fool, it will be well done before you put your
teeth in it.

Fool. My teeth are growing long with the hunger.

Blind Man. I'll tell you a story—the kings have story-
tellers while they are waiting for their dinner—I
will tell you a story with a fight in it, a story with a
champion in it, and a ship and a queen's son that
has his mind set on killing somebody that you and
I know.

Fool. Who is that? Who is he coming to kill?

Blind Man. Wait, now, till you hear. When you were
stealing the fowl, I was lying in a hole in the sand,
and I heard three men coming with a shuffling sort
of noise. They were wounded and groaning.

Fool. Go on. Tell me about the fight.

Blind Man. There had been a fight, a great fight, a
tremendous great fight. A young man had landed on
the shore, the guardians of the shore had asked his
name, and he had refused to tell it, and he had killed
one, and others had run away.

Fool. That's enough. Come on now to the fowl. I wish
it was bigger. I wish it was as big as a goose.

Blind Man. Hush! I haven't told you all. I know who
that young man is. I heard the men who were running away say he had red hair, that he had come
from Aoife's country, that he was coming to kill
Cuchulain.

Fool. Nobody can do that.

[*To a tune*]
Cuchulain has killed kings,
Kings and sons of kings,
Dragons out of the water,
And witches out of the air,
Banachas and Bonachas and people of the woods.

Blind Man. Hush! hush!

Fool [*still singing*].
Witches that steal the milk,
Fomor that steal the children,
Hags that have heads like hares,
Hares that have claws like witches,
All riding a-cock-horse

[*Spoken*]
Out of the very bottom of the bitter black North.

Blind Man. Hush, I say!

Fool. Does Cuchulain know that he is coming to kill him?

Blind Man. How would he know that with his head in the clouds? He doesn't care for common fighting. Why would he put himself out, and nobody in it but that young man? Now if it were a white fawn that might turn into a queen before morning—

Fool. Come to the fowl. I wish it was as big as a pig; a fowl with goose grease and pig's crackling.

Blind Man. No hurry, no hurry. I know whose son it is. I wouldn't tell anybody else, but I will tell you,—a secret is better to you than your dinner. You like being told secrets.

Fool. Tell me the secret.

Blind Man. That young man is Aoife's son. I am sure
it is Aoife's son, it flows in upon me that it is Aoife's
son. You have often heard me talking of Aoife, the
great woman-fighter Cuchulain got the mastery over
in the North?

Fool. I know, I know. She is one of those cross queens
that live in hungry Scotland.

Blind Man. I am sure it is her son. I was in Aoife's
country for a long time.

Fool. That was before you were blinded for putting a
curse upon the wind.

Blind Man. There was a boy in her house that had her
own red colour on him, and everybody said he was
to be brought up to kill Cuchulain, that she hated
Cuchulain. She used to put a helmet on a pillar-
stone and call it Cuchulain and set him casting at it.
There is a step outside—Cuchulain's step.

> [*Cuchulain passes by in the mist outside the big door.*

Fool. Where is Cuchulain going?

Blind Man. He is going to meet Conchubar that has
bidden him to take the oath.

Fool. Ah, an oath, Blind Man. How can I remember so
many things at once? Who is going to take an oath?

Blind Man. Cuchulain is going to take an oath to Conchubar who is High King.

Fool. What a mix-up you make of everything, Blind
Man! You were telling me one story, and now you
are telling me another story. . . . How can I get the
hang of it at the end if you mix everything at the
beginning? Wait till I settle it out. There now, there's

Cuchulain [*he points to one foot*], and there is the young
man [*he points to the other foot*] that is coming to kill
him, and Cuchulain doesn't know. But where's Conchubar? [*Takes bag from side.*] That's Conchubar with
all his riches—Cuchulain, young man, Conchubar.—
And where's Aoife? [*Throws up cap.*] There is Aoife,
high up on the mountains in high hungry Scotland.
Maybe it is not true after all. Maybe it was your
own making up. It's many a time you cheated me
before with your lies. Come to the cooking-pot, my
stomach is pinched and rusty. Would you have it to
be creaking like a gate?

Blind Man. I tell you it's true. And more than that is
true. If you listen to what I say, you'll forget your
stomach.

Fool. I won't.

Blind Man. Listen. I know who the young man's father
is, but I won't say. I would be afraid to say. Ah,
Fool, you would forget everything if you could know
who the young man's father is.

Fool. Who is it? Tell me now quick, or I'll shake you.
Come, out with it, or I'll shake you.
                          [*A murmur of voices in the distance.*

Blind Man. Wait, wait. There's somebody coming. . . .
It is Cuchulain is coming. He's coming back with
the High King. Go and ask Cuchulain. He'll tell
you. It's little you'll care about the cooking-pot
when you have asked Cuchulain that . . .
                          [*Blind Man goes out by side door.*

Fool. I'll ask him. Cuchulain will know. He was in
Aoife's country. [*Goes up stage.*] I'll ask him. [*Turns*

and goes down stage.] But, no, I won't ask him, I would be afraid. [*Going up again.*] Yes, I will ask him. What harm in asking? The Blind Man said I was to ask him. [*Going down.*] No, no. I'll not ask him. He might kill me. I have but killed hens and geese and pigs. He has killed kings. [*Goes up again almost to big door.*] Who says I'm afraid? I'm not afraid. I'm no coward. I'll ask him. No, no, Cuchulain, I'm not going to ask you.

> He has killed kings,
> Kings and the sons of kings,
> Dragons out of the water,
> And witches out of the air,

Banachas and Bonachas and people of the woods.

[*Fool goes out by side door, the last words being heard outside. Cuchulain and Conchubar enter through the big door at the back. While they are still outside, Cuchulain's voice is heard raised in anger. He is a dark man, something over forty years of age. Conchubar is much older and carries a long staff, elaborately carved or with an elaborate gold handle.*

Cuchulain. Because I have killed men without your bidding
And have rewarded others at my own pleasure,
Because of half a score of trifling things,
You'd lay this oath upon me, and now—and now
You add another pebble to the heap,
And I must be your man, well-nigh your bondsman,
Because a youngster out of Aoife's country
Has found the shore ill-guarded.

Conchubar.   He came to land

While you were somewhere out of sight and hearing,
Hunting or dancing with your wild companions.

Cuchulain. He can be driven out. I'll not be bound.
I'll dance or hunt, or quarrel or make love,
Wherever and whenever I've a mind to.
If time had not put water in your blood,
You never would have thought it.

Conchubar.   I would leave
A strong and settled country to my children.

Cuchulain. And I must be obedient in all things;
Give up my will to yours; go where you please;
Come when you call; sit at the council-board
Among the unshapely bodies of old men;
I whose mere name has kept this country safe,
I that in early days have driven out
Maeve of Cruachan and the northern pirates,
The hundred kings of Sorcha, and the kings
Out of the Garden in the East of the World.
Must I, that held you on the throne when all
Had pulled you from it, swear obedience
As if I were some cattle-raising king?
Are my shins speckled with the heat of the fire,
Or have my hands no skill but to make figures
Upon the ashes with a stick? Am I
So slack and idle that I need a whip
Before I serve you?

Conchubar.   No, no whip, Cuchulain,
But every day my children come and say:
'This man is growing harder to endure.
How can we be at safety with this man
That nobody can buy or bid or bind?

We shall be at his mercy when you are gone;
He burns the earth as if he were a fire,
And time can never touch him.'

Cuchulain.   And so the tale
Grows finer yet; and I am to obey
Whatever child you set upon the throne,
As if it were yourself!

Conchubar.   Most certainly.
I am High King, my son shall be High King;
And you for all the wildness of your blood,
And though your father came out of the sun,
Are but a little king and weigh but light
In anything that touches government,
If put into the balance with my children.

Cuchulain. It's well that we should speak our minds
      out plainly,
For when we die we shall be spoken of
In many countries. We in our young days
Have seen the heavens like a burning cloud
Brooding upon the world, and being more
Than men can be now that cloud's lifted up,
We should be the more truthful. Conchubar,
I do not like your children—they have no pith,
No marrow in their bones, and will lie soft
Where you and I lie hard.

Conchubar.   You rail at them
Because you have no children of your own.

Cuchulain. I think myself most lucky that I leave
No pallid ghost or mockery of a man
To drift and mutter in the corridors
Where I have laughed and sung.

Conchubar.   That is not true,
   For all your boasting of the truth between us;
   For there is no man having house and lands,
   That have been in the one family, called
   By that one family's name for centuries,
   But is made miserable if he know
   They are to pass into a stranger's keeping,
   As yours will pass.

Cuchulain.   The most of men feel that,
   But you and I leave names upon the harp.

Conchubar. You play with arguments as lawyers do,
   And put no heart in them. I know your thoughts,
   For we have slept under the one cloak and drunk
   From the one wine-cup. I know you to the bone,
   I have heard you cry, aye, in your very sleep,
   'I have no son', and with such bitterness
   That I have gone upon my knees and prayed
   That it might be amended.

Cuchulain.   For you thought
   That I should be as biddable as others
   Had I their reason for it; but that's not true;
   For I would need a weightier argument
   Than one that marred me in the copying,
   As I have that clean hawk out of the air
   That, as men say, begot this body of mine
   Upon a mortal woman.

Conchubar.   Now as ever
   You mock at every reasonable hope,
   And would have nothing, or impossible things.
   What eye has ever looked upon the child
   Would satisfy a mind like that?

Cuchulain.   I would leave
  My house and name to none that would not face
  Even myself in battle.

Conchubar.   Being swift of foot,
  And making light of every common chance,
  You should have overtaken on the hills
  Some daughter of the air, or on the shore
  A daughter of the Country-under-Wave.

Cuchulain. I am not blasphemous.

Conchubar.   Yet you despise
  Our queens, and would not call a child your own,
  If one of them had borne him.

Cuchulain.   I have not said it.

Conchubar. Ah! I remember I have heard you boast,
  When the ale was in your blood, that there was one
  In Scotland, where you had learnt the trade of war,
  That had a stone-pale cheek and red-brown hair;
  And that although you had loved other women,
  You'd sooner that fierce woman of the camp
  Bore you a son than any queen among them.

Cuchulain. You call her a 'fierce woman of the camp',
  For, having lived among the spinning-wheels,
  You'd have no woman near that would not say,
  'Ah! how wise!' 'What will you have for supper?'
  'What shall I wear that I may please you, sir?'
  And keep that humming through the day and night
  For ever. A fierce woman of the camp!
  But I am getting angry about nothing.
  You have never seen her. Ah! Conchubar, had you
      seen her
  With that high, laughing, turbulent head of hers

Thrown backward, and the bowstring at her ear,
Or sitting at the fire with those grave eyes
Full of good counsel as it were with wine,
Or when love ran through all the lineaments
Of her wild body—although she had no child,
None other had all beauty, queen or lover,
Or was so fitted to give birth to kings.

Conchubar. There's nothing I can say but drifts you
        farther
From the one weighty matter. That very woman—
For I know well that you are praising Aoife—
Now hates you and will leave no subtlety
Unknotted that might run into a noose
About your throat, no army in idleness
That might bring ruin on this land you serve.

Cuchulain. No wonder in that, no wonder at all in that.
I never have known love but as a kiss
In the mid-battle, and a difficult truce
Of oil and water, candles and dark night,
Hillside and hollow, the hot-footed sun
And the cold, sliding, slippery-footed moon—
A brief forgiveness between opposites
That have been hatreds for three times the age
Of this long-'stablished ground.

Conchubar.   Listen to me.
Aoife makes war on us, and every day
Our enemies grow greater and beat the walls
More bitterly, and you within the walls
Are every day more turbulent; and yet,
When I would speak about these things, your fancy
Runs as it were a swallow on the wind.

G

[*Outside the door in the blue light of the sea-mist are
many old and young Kings; amongst them are three
Women, two of whom carry a bowl of fire. The third,
in what follows, puts from time to time fragrant
herbs into the fire so that it flickers up into brighter
flame.*

Look at the door and what men gather there—
Old counsellors that steer the land with me,
And younger kings, the dancers and harp-players
That follow in your tumults, and all these
Are held there by the one anxiety.
Will you be bound into obedience
And so make this land safe for them and theirs?
You are but half a king and I but half;
I need your might of hand and burning heart,
And you my wisdom.

Cuchulain [*going near to door*]. Nestlings of a high nest,
Hawks that have followed me into the air
And looked upon the sun, we'll out of this
And sail upon the wind once more. This king
Would have me take an oath to do his will,
And having listened to his tune from morning,
I will no more of it. Run to the stable
And set the horses to the chariot-pole,
And send a messenger to the harp-players.
We'll find a level place among the woods,
And dance awhile.

A Young King.   Cuchulain, take the oath.
There is none here that would not have you take it.

Cuchulain. You'd have me take it? Are you of one
mind?

The Kings. All, all, all, all!

A Young King.   Do what the High King bids you.

Conchubar. There is not one but dreads this turbulence
  Now that they're settled men.

Cuchulain.   Are you so changed,
  Or have I grown more dangerous of late?
  But that's not it. I understand it all.
  It's you that have changed. You've wives and
      children now,
  And for that reason cannot follow one
  That lives like a bird's flight from tree to tree.—
  It's time the years put water in my blood
  And drowned the wildness of it, for all's changed,
  But that unchanged.—I'll take what oath you will:
  The moon, the sun, the water, light, or air,
  I do not care how binding.

Conchubar.   On this fire
  That has been lighted from your hearth and mine;
  The older men shall be my witnesses,
  The younger, yours. The holders of the fire
  Shall purify the thresholds of the house
  With waving fire, and shut the outer door,
  According to the custom; and sing rhyme
  That has come down from the old law-makers
  To blow the witches out. Considering
  That the wild will of man could be oath-bound,
  But that a woman's could not, they bid us sing
  Against the will of woman at its wildest
  In the Shape-Changers that run upon the wind.
                    [*Conchubar has gone on to his throne.*

The Women. [*They sing in a very low voice after the first*
few words so that the others all but drown their words.
 May this fire have driven out
 The Shape-Changers that can put
 Ruin on a great king's house
 Until all be ruinous.
 Names whereby a man has known
 The threshold and the hearthstone,
 Gather on the wind and drive
 The women none can kiss and thrive,
 For they are but whirling wind,
 Out of memory and mind.
 They would make a prince decay
 With light images of clay
 Planted in the running wave;
 Or, for many shapes they have,
 They would change them into hounds
 Until he had died of his wounds,
 Though the change were but a whim;
 Or they'd hurl a spell at him,
 That he follow with desire
 Bodies that can never tire
 Or grow kind, for they anoint
 All their bodies, joint by joint,
 With a miracle-working juice
 That is made out of the grease
 Of the ungoverned unicorn.
 But the man is thrice forlorn,
 Emptied, ruined, wracked, and lost,
 That they follow, for at most
 They will give him kiss for kiss
 While they murmur, 'After this
 Hatred may be sweet to the taste'.

Those wild hands that have embraced
All his body can but shove
At the burning wheel of love
Till the side of hate comes up.
Therefore in this ancient cup
May the sword-blades drink their fill
Of the home-brew there, until
They will have for masters none
But the threshold and hearthstone.

Cuchulain [speaking, while they are singing]. I'll take and
        keep this oath, and from this day
  I shall be what you please, my chicks, my nestlings.
  Yet I had thought you were of those that praised
  Whatever life could make the pulse run quickly,
  Even though it were brief, and that you held
  That a free gift was better than a forced.—
  But that's all over.—I will keep it, too;
  I never gave a gift and took it again.
  If the wild horse should break the chariot-pole,
  It would be punished. Should that be in the oath?
    [Two of the Women, still singing, crouch in front of
        him holding the bowl over their heads. He spreads his
        hands over the flame.
  I swear to be obedient in all things
  To Conchubar, and to uphold his children.

Conchubar. We are one being, as these flames are one:
  I give my wisdom, and I take your strength.
  Now thrust the swords into the flame, and pray
  That they may serve the threshold and the hearthstone
  With faithful service.
    [The Kings kneel in a semicircle before the two Women
        and Cuchulain, who thrusts his sword into the flame.

> *They all put the points of their swords into the flame.*
> *The third Woman is at the back near the big door.*

Cuchulain.   O pure, glittering ones
That should be more than wife or friend or mistress,
Give us the enduring will, the unquenchable hope,
The friendliness of the sword!—
> [*The song grows louder, and the last words ring out*
> *clearly. There is a loud knocking at the door, and a*
> *cry of* 'Open! open!'

Conchubar. Some king that has been loitering on the
        way.
Open the door, for I would have all know
That the oath's finished and Cuchulain bound,
And that the swords are drinking up the flame.
> [*The door is opened by the third Woman, and a Young*
> *Man with a drawn sword enters.*

Young Man. I am of Aoife's country.
> [*The Kings rush towards him. Cuchulain throws himself*
> *between.*

Cuchulain.   Put up your swords.
He is but one. Aoife is far away.

Young Man. I have come alone into the midst of you
To weigh this sword against Cuchulain's sword.

Conchubar. And are you noble? for if of common seed,
You cannot weigh your sword against his sword
But in mixed battle.

Young Man.   I am under bonds
To tell my name to no man; but it's noble.

Conchubar. But I would know your name and not your
        bonds.

You cannot speak in the Assembly House,
If you are not noble.

First Old King.   Answer the High King!

Young Man. I will give no other proof than the hawk
gives
That it's no sparrow!
                    [*He is silent for a moment, then speaks to all.*
                              Yet look upon me, kings.
I, too, am of that ancient seed, and carry
The signs about this body and in these bones.

Cuchulain. To have shown the hawk's grey feather is
enough,
And you speak highly, too. Give me that helmet.
I'd thought they had grown weary sending cham-
pions.
That sword and belt will do. This fighting's wel-
come.
The High King there has promised me his wisdom;
But the hawk's sleepy till its well-beloved
Cries out amid the acorns, or it has seen
Its enemy like a speck upon the sun.
What's wisdom to the hawk, when that clear eye
Is burning nearer up in the high air?
    [*Looks hard at Young Man; then comes down steps and
    grasps Young Man by shoulder.*
Hither into the light.
[*To Conchubar.*]   The very tint
Of her that I was speaking of but now.
Not a pin's difference.
[*To Young Man.*]   You are from the North,
Where there are many that have that tint of hair—

Red-brown, the light red-brown. Come nearer, boy,
For I would have another look at you.
There's more likeness—a pale, a stone-pale cheek.
What brought you, boy? Have you no fear of death?

Young Man. Whether I live or die is in the gods' hands.

Cuchulain. That is all words, all words; a young man's
    talk.
I am their plough, their harrow, their very strength;
For he that's in the sun begot this body
Upon a mortal woman, and I have heard tell
It seemed as if he had outrun the moon
That he must follow always through waste heaven,
He loved so happily. He'll be but slow
To break a tree that was so sweetly planted.
Let's see that arm. I'll see it if I choose.
That arm had a good father and a good mother,
But it is not like this.

Young Man.   You are mocking me;
You think I am not worthy to be fought.
But I'll not wrangle but with this talkative knife.

Cuchulain. Put up your sword; I am not mocking you.
I'd have you for my friend, but if it's not
Because you have a hot heart and a cold eye,
I cannot tell the reason.
[*To Conchubar.*]   He has got her fierceness,
And nobody is as fierce as those pale women.
But I will keep him with me, Conchubar,
That he may set my memory upon her
When the day's fading.—You will stop with us,
And we will hunt the deer and the wild bulls;
And, when we have grown weary, light our fires
Between the wood and water, or on some mountain

Where the Shape-Changers of the morning come.
The High King there would make a mock of me
Because I did not take a wife among them.
Why do you hang your head? It's a good life:
The head grows prouder in the light of the dawn,
And friendship thickens in the murmuring dark
Where the spare hazels meet the wool-white foam.
But I can see there's no more need for words
And that you'll be my friend from this day out.

Conchubar. He has come hither not in his own name
But in Queen Aoife's, and has challenged us
In challenging the foremost man of us all.

Cuchulain. Well, well, what matter?

Conchubar.   You think it does not matter,
And that a fancy lighter than the air,
A whim of the moment, has more matter in it.
For having none that shall reign after you,
You cannot think as I do, who would leave
A throne too high for insult.

Cuchulain.   Let your children
Re-mortar their inheritance, as we have,
And put more muscle on.—I'll give you gifts,
But I'd have something too—that arm-ring, boy.
We'll have this quarrel out when you are older.

Young Man. There is no man I'd sooner have my friend
Than you, whose name has gone about the world
As if it had been the wind; but Aoife'd say
I had turned coward.

Cuchulain.   I will give you gifts
That Aoife'll know, and all her people know,
To have come from me.   [*Showing cloak.*

                    My father gave me this.
He came to try me, rising up at dawn
Out of the cold dark of the rich sea.
He challenged me to battle, but before
My sword had touched his sword, told me his name,
Gave me this cloak, and vanished. It was woven
By women of the Country-under-Wave
Out of the fleeces of the sea. O! tell her
I was afraid, or tell her what you will.
No; tell her that I heard a raven croak
On the north side of the house, and was afraid.

Conchubar. Some witch of the air has troubled Cuchu-
    lain's mind.

Cuchulain. No witchcraft. His head is like a woman's
    head
  I had a fancy for.

Conchubar.   A witch of the air
  Can make a leaf confound us with memories.
  They run upon the wind and hurl the spells
  That make us nothing, out of the invisible wind.
  They have gone to school to learn the trick of it.

Cuchulain. No, no—there's nothing out of common
    here;
  The winds are innocent.—That arm-ring, boy.

A King. If I've your leave I'll take this challenge up.

Another King. No, give it me, High King, for this wild
    Aoife
  Has carried off my slaves.

Another King.   No, give it me,
  For she has harried me in house and herd.

Another King. I claim this fight.

Other Kings [*together*].   And I! And I! And I!

Cuchulain. Back! back! Put up your swords! Put up
    your swords!
  There's none alive that shall accept a challenge
  I have refused. Laegaire, put up your sword!

Young Man. No, let them come. If they've a mind for it,
  I'll try it out with any two together.

Cuchulain. That's spoken as I'd have spoken it at your
    age.
  But you are in my house. Whatever man
  Would fight with you shall fight it out with me.
  They're dumb, they're dumb. How many of you
    would meet   [*Draws sword.*
  This mutterer, this old whistler, this sand-piper,
  This edge that's greyer than the tide, this mouse
  That's gnawing at the timbers of the world,
  This, this—Boy, I would meet them all in arms
  If I'd a son like you. He would avenge me
  When I have withstood for the last time the men
  Whose fathers, brothers, sons, and friends I have
    killed
  Upholding Conchubar, when the four provinces
  Have gathered with the ravens over them.
  But I'd need no avenger. You and I
  Would scatter them like water from a dish.

Young Man. We'll stand by one another from this out.
  Here is the ring.

Cuchulain.   No, turn and turn about.
  But my turn's first because I am the older.
                    [*Spreading out cloak.*
  Nine queens out of the Country-under-Wave

Have woven it with the fleeces of the sea
And they were long embroidering at it.—Boy,
If I had fought my father, he'd have killed me,
As certainly as if I had a son
And fought with him, I should be deadly to him;
For the old fiery fountains are far off
And every day there is less heat o' the blood.

Conchubar [*in a loud voice*]. No more of this. I will not
    have this friendship.
    Cuchulain is my man, and I forbid it.
    He shall not go unfought, for I myself—

Cuchulain. I will not have it.

Conchubar.   You lay commands on me?

Cuchulain [*seizing Conchubar*]. You shall not stir, High
    King. I'll hold you there.

Conchubar. Witchcraft has maddened you.

The Kings [*shouting*].   Yes, witchcraft! witchcraft!

First Old King. Some witch has worked upon your
    mind, Cuchulain.
    The head of that young man seemed like a woman's
    You'd had a fancy for. Then of a sudden
    You laid your hands on the High King himself!

Cuchulain. And laid my hands on the High King him-
    self?

Conchubar. Some witch is floating in the air above us.

Cuchulain. Yes, witchcraft! witchcraft! Witches of the
    air!
    [*To Young Man.*] Why did you? Who was it set you
    to this work?
    Out, out! I say, for now it's sword on sword!

Young Man. But . . . but I did not.

Cuchulain.   Out, I say, out, out!

[*Young Man goes out followed by Cuchulain. The Kings
follow them out with confused cries, and words one
can hardly hear because of the noise. Some cry,
'Quicker, quicker!' 'Why are you so long at the
door?' 'We'll be too late!' 'Have they begun to
fight?' 'Can you see if they are fighting?' and so
on. Their voices drown each other. The three Women
are left alone.*

First Woman. I have seen, I have seen!

Second Woman.   What do you cry aloud?

First Woman. The Ever-living have shown me what's
to come.

Third Woman. How? Where?

First Woman.   In the ashes of the bowl.

Second Woman. While you were holding it between
your hands?

Third Woman. Speak quickly!

First Woman.   I have seen Cuchulain's roof-tree
Leap into fire, and the walls split and blacken.

Second Woman. Cuchulain has gone out to die.

Third Woman.   O! O!

Second Woman. Who could have thought that one so
great as he
Should meet his end at this unnoted sword!

First Woman. Life drifts between a fool and a blind man
To the end, and nobody can know his end.

Second Woman. Come, look upon the quenching of this greatness.

    [*The other two go to the door, but they stop for a moment upon the threshold and wail.*

First Woman. No crying out, for there'll be need of cries

    And rending of the hair when it's all finished.

    [*The Women go out. There is the sound of clashing swords from time to time during what follows.*

    Enter the Fool, dragging the Blind Man.

Fool. You have eaten it, you have eaten it! You have left me nothing but the bones.

    [*He throws Blind Man down by big chair.*

Blind Man. O, that I should have to endure such a plague! O, I ache all over! O, I am pulled to pieces! This is the way you pay me all the good I have done you.

Fool. You have eaten it! You have told me lies. I might have known you had eaten it when I saw your slow, sleepy walk. Lie there till the kings come. O, I will tell Conchubar and Cuchulain and all the kings about you!

Blind Man. What would have happened to you but for me, and you without your wits? If I did not take care of you, what would you do for food and warmth?

Fool. You take care of me? You stay safe, and send me into every kind of danger. You sent me down the cliff for gulls' eggs while you warmed your blind eyes in the sun; and then you ate all that were good for food. You left me the eggs that were neither egg nor bird. [*Blind Man tries to rise; Fool makes him lie down again.*] Keep quiet now, till I shut the door. There is some noise outside—a high vexing noise, so that I can't be listening to myself. [*Shuts the big door.*] Why can't they be quiet? why can't they be quiet? [*Blind Man tries to get away.*] Ah! you would get away, would you? [*Follows Blind Man and brings him back.*] Lie there! lie there! No, you won't get away! Lie there till the kings come. I'll tell them all about you. I will tell it all. How you sit warming yourself, when you have made me light a fire of sticks, while I sit blowing it with my mouth. Do you not always make me take the windy side of the bush when it blows, and the rainy side when it rains?

Blind Man. O, good Fool! listen to me. Think of the care I have taken of you. I have brought you to many a warm hearth, where there was a good welcome for you, but you would not stay there; you were always wandering about.

Fool. The last time you brought me in, it was not I who wandered away, but you that got put out because you took the crubeen out of the pot when nobody was looking. Keep quiet, now!

Cuchulain [*rushing in*]. Witchcraft! There is no witchcraft on the earth, or among the witches of the air, that these hands cannot break.

Fool. Listen to me, Cuchulain. I left him turning the fowl at the fire. He ate it all, though I had stolen it. He left me nothing but the feathers.

Cuchulain. Fill me a horn of ale!

Blind Man. I gave him what he likes best. You do not know how vain this Fool is. He likes nothing so well as a feather.

Fool. He left me nothing but the bones and feathers. Nothing but the feathers, though I had stolen it.

Cuchulain. Give me that horn. Quarrels here, too! [*Drinks.*] What is there between you two that is worth a quarrel? Out with it!

Blind Man. Where would he be but for me? I must be always thinking—thinking to get food for the two of us, and when we've got it, if the moon is at the full or the tide on the turn, he'll leave the rabbit in the snare till it is full of maggots, or let the trout slip back through his hands into the stream.
   [*The Fool has begun singing while the Blind Man is speaking.*

Fool [*singing*].
        When you were an acorn on the tree-top,
           Then was I an eagle-cock;
        Now that you are a withered old block,
           Still am I an eagle-cock.

Blind Man. Listen to him, now. That's the sort of talk I have to put up with day out, day in.
   [*The Fool is putting the feathers into his hair. Cuchulain takes a handful of feathers out of a heap the Fool has on the bench beside him, and out of the Fool's hair, and begins to wipe the blood from his sword with them.*

Fool. He has taken my feathers to wipe his sword. It is blood that he is wiping from his sword.

Cuchulain [*goes up to door at back and throws away feathers*]. They are standing about his body. They will not awaken him, for all his witchcraft.

Blind Man. It is that young champion that he has killed. He that came out of Aoife's country.

Cuchulain. He thought to have saved himself with witchcraft.

Fool. That Blind Man there said he would kill you. He came from Aoife's country to kill you. That Blind Man said they had taught him every kind of weapon that he might do it. But I always knew that you would kill him.

Cuchulain [*to the Blind Man*]. You knew him, then?

Blind Man. I saw him, when I had my eyes, in Aoife's country.

Cuchulain. You were in Aoife's country?

Blind Man. I knew him and his mother there.

Cuchulain. He was about to speak of her when he died.

Blind Man. He was a queen's son.

Cuchulain. What queen? what queen? [*Seizes Blind Man, who is now sitting upon the bench.*] Was it Scathach? There were many queens. All the rulers there were queens.

Blind Man. No, not Scathach.

Cuchulain. It was Uathach, then? Speak! speak!

Blind Man. I cannot speak; you are clutching me too tightly. [*Cuchulain lets him go.*] I cannot remember who it was. I am not certain. It was some queen.

Fool. He said a while ago that the young man was Aoife's son.

Cuchulain. She? No, no! She had no son when I was there.

Fool. That Blind Man there said that she owned him for her son.

H

Cuchulain. I had rather he had been some other woman's son. What father had he? A soldier out of Alba? She was an amorous woman—a proud, pale, amorous woman.

Blind Man. None knew whose son he was.

Cuchulain. None knew! Did you know, old listener at doors?

Blind Man. No, no; I knew nothing.

Fool. He said a while ago that he heard Aoife boast that she'd never but the one lover, and he the only man that had overcome her in battle.   [*Pause.*

Blind Man. Somebody is trembling, Fool! The bench is shaking. Why are you trembling? Is Cuchulain going to hurt us? It was not I who told you, Cuchulain.

Fool. It is Cuchulain who is trembling. It is Cuchulain who is shaking the bench.

Blind Man. It is his own son he has slain.

Cuchulain. 'Twas they that did it, the pale windy people.
Where? where? where? My sword against the thunder!
But no, for they have always been my friends;
And though they love to blow a smoking coal
Till it's all flame, the wars they blow aflame
Are full of glory, and heart-uplifting pride,
And not like this. The wars they love awaken
Old fingers and the sleepy strings of harps.
Who did it then? Are you afraid? Speak out!
For I have put you under my protection,
And will reward you well. Dubthach the Chafer?
He'd an old grudge. No, for he is with Maeve.

Laegaire did it! Why do you not speak?
What is this house? [*Pause.*] Now I remember all.
    [*Comes before Conchubar's chair, and strikes out with*
      his sword, as if Conchubar was sitting upon it.
'Twas you who did it—you who sat up there
With your old rod of kingship, like a magpie
Nursing a stolen spoon. No, not a magpie,
A maggot that is eating up the earth!
Yes, but a magpie, for he's flown away.
Where did he fly to?

Blind Man.   He is outside the door.

Cuchulain. Outside the door?

Blind Man.   Between the door and the sea.

Cuchulain. Conchubar, Conchubar! the sword into your
    heart!
    [*He rushes out. Pause. Fool creeps up to the big door and*
      looks after him.

Fool. He is going up to King Conchubar. They are all
about the young man. No, no, he is standing still.
There is a great wave going to break, and he is looking at it. Ah! now he is running down to the sea,
but he is holding up his sword as if he were going
into a fight. [*Pause.*] Well struck! well struck!

Blind Man. What is he doing now?

Fool. O! he is fighting the waves!

Blind Man. He sees King Conchubar's crown on every
one of them.

Fool. There, he has struck at a big one! He has struck
the crown off it; he has made the foam fly. There
again, another big one!

Blind Man. Where are the kings? What are the kings doing?

Fool. They are shouting and running down to the shore, and the people are running out of the houses. They are all running.

Blind Man. You say they are running out of the houses? There will be nobody left in the houses. Listen, Fool!

Fool. There, he is down! He is up again. He is going out in the deep water. There is a big wave. It has gone over him. I cannot see him now. He has killed kings and giants, but the waves have mastered him, the waves have mastered him!

Blind Man. Come here, Fool!

Fool. The waves have mastered him.

Blind Man. Come here!

Fool. The waves have mastered him.

Blind Man. Come here, I say.

Fool [*coming towards him, but looking backwards towards the door*]. What is it?

Blind Man. There will be nobody in the houses. Come this way; come quickly! The ovens will be full. We will put our hands into the ovens.   [*They go out.*

THE END

DEIRDRE

1907

TO

MRS. PATRICK CAMPBELL

who in the generosity of her genius has played my
Deirdre in Dublin and London with the Abbey
Company, as well as with her own people, and

IN MEMORY OF

ROBERT GREGORY

who designed the beautiful scene she played it in.

DEIRDRE

PERSONS IN THE PLAY

Musicians
Fergus, *an old man*
Naoise, *a young king*
Deirdre, *his queen*

A Dark-faced Messenger
Conchubar (*pronounced* Conochar),
   *the old King of Ulad, who is still
   strong and vigorous*
A Dark-faced Executioner

*A Guest-house in a wood. It is a rough house of timber;
through the doors and some of the windows one can see the great
spaces of the wood, the sky dimming, night closing in. But a
window to the left shows the thick leaves of a coppice; the
landscape suggests silence and loneliness. There is a door to
right and left, and through the side windows one can see
anybody who approaches either door, a moment before he
enters. In the centre, a part of the house is curtained off; the
curtains are drawn. There are unlighted torches in brackets on
the walls. There is, at one side, a small table with a chess-
board and chessmen upon it. At the other side of the room there
is a brazier with a fire; two women, with musical instruments beside them, crouch about the brazier: they are comely
women of about forty. Another woman, who carries a stringed
instrument, enters hurriedly; she speaks, at first standing in
the doorway.*

First Musician. I have a story right, my wanderers,
   That has so mixed with fable in our songs
   That all seemed fabulous. We are come, by chance,
   Into King Conchubar's country, and this house

Is an old guest-house built for travellers
From the seashore to Conchubar's royal house,
And there are certain hills among these woods
And there Queen Deirdre grew.

Second Musician.   That famous queen
Who has been wandering with her lover Naoise,
Somewhere beyond the edges of the world?

First Musician [*going nearer to the brazier*]. Some dozen
    years ago, King Conchubar found
A house upon a hillside in this wood,
And there a child with an old witch to nurse her,
And nobody to say if she were human,
Or of the gods, or anything at all
Of who she was or why she was hidden there,
But that she'd too much beauty for good luck.
He went up thither daily, till at last
She put on womanhood, and he lost peace,
And Deirdre's tale began. The King was old.
A month or so before the marriage day,
A young man, in the laughing scorn of his
    youth,
Naoise, the son of Usna, climbed up there,
And having wooed, or, as some say, been wooed,
Carried her off.

Second Musician.   The tale were well enough
Had it a finish.

First Musician.   Hush! I have more to tell;
But gather close about that I may whisper
The secrets of a king.

Second Musician.   There's none to hear!

First Musician. I have been to Conchubar's house and
    followed up
A crowd of servants going out and in
With loads upon their heads: embroideries
To hang upon the walls, or new-mown rushes
To strew upon the floors, and came at length
To a great room.

Second Musician.   Be silent; there are steps!

*Enter Fergus, an old man, who moves about from door to
    window excitedly through what follows.*

Fergus. I thought to find a message from the King.
You are musicians by these instruments,
And if as seems—for you are comely women—
You can praise love, you'll have the best of luck,
For there'll be two, before the night is in,
That bargained for their love, and paid for it
All that men value. You have but the time
To weigh a happy music with a sad,
To find what is most pleasing to a lover,
Before the son of Usna and his queen
Have passed this threshold.

First Musician.   Deirdre and her man!

Fergus. I was to have found a message in this house,
And ran to meet it. Is there no messenger
From Conchubar to Fergus, son of Roigh?

First Musician. Are Deirdre and her lover tired of life?

Fergus. You are not of this country, or you'd know
That they are in my charge and all forgiven.

First Musician. We have no country but the roads of the
    world.

Fergus. Then you should know that all things change
  in the world,
 And hatred turns to love and love to hate,
 And even kings forgive.

First Musician.   An old man's love
 Who casts no second line is hard to cure;
 His jealousy is like his love.

Fergus.   And that's but true.
 You have learned something in your wanderings.
 He was so hard to cure that the whole court,
 But I alone, thought it impossible;
 Yet after I had urged it at all seasons,
 I had my way, and all's forgiven now;
 And you shall speak the welcome and the joy
 That I lack tongue for.

First Musician.   Yet old men are jealous.

Fergus [*going to door*]. I am Conchubar's near friend, and
  that weighed somewhat,
 And it was policy to pardon them.
 The need of some young, famous, popular man
 To lead the troops, the murmur of the crowd,
 And his own natural impulse, urged him to it.
 They have been wandering half a dozen years.

First Musician. And yet old men are jealous.

Fergus [*coming from door*].   Sing the more sweetly
 Because, though age is arid as a bone,
 This man has flowered. I've need of music, too;
 If this grey head would suffer no reproach,
 I'd dance and sing—

[*Dark-faced men with strange, barbaric dress and arms
    begin to pass by the doors and windows. They pass one
    by one and in silence.*

                                    and dance till the hour ran out,
Because I have accomplished this good deed.

First Musician. Look there—there at the window, those
        dark men,
    With murderous and outlandish-looking arms—
    They've been about the house all day.

Fergus [*looking after them*].   What are you?
    Where do you come from, who is it sent you here?

First Musician. They will not answer you.

Fergus.   They do not hear.

First Musician. Forgive my open speech, but to these
        eyes
    That have seen many lands they are such men
    As kings will gather for a murderous task
    That neither bribes, commands, nor promises
    Can bring their people to.

Fergus.   And that is why
    You harped upon an old man's jealousy.
    A trifle sets you quaking. Conchubar's fame
    Brings merchandise on every wind that blows.
    They may have brought him Libyan dragon-skin,
    Or the ivory of the fierce unicorn.

First Musician. If these be merchants, I have seen the
        goods
    They have brought to Conchubar, and understood
    His murderous purpose.

Fergus.   Murderous, you say?

Why, what new gossip of the roads is this?
But I'll not hear.

First Musician.   It may be life or death.
There is a room in Conchubar's house, and there——

Fergus. Be silent, or I'll drive you from the door.
There's many a one that would do more than that,
And make it prison, or death, or banishment
To slander the High King.
                    [*Suddenly restraining himself and speaking gently.*
                              He is my friend;
I have his oath, and I am well content.
I have known his mind as if it were my own
These many years, and there is none alive
Shall buzz against him, and I there to stop it.
I know myself, and him, and your wild thought
Fed on extravagant poetry, and lit
By such a dazzle of old fabulous tales
That common things are lost, and all that's strange
Is true because 'twere pity if it were not.
                              [*Going to the door again.*
Quick! quick! your instruments! they are coming
     now.
I hear the hoofs a-clatter. Begin that song!
But what is it to be? I'd have them hear
A music foaming up out of the house
Like wine out of a cup. Come now, a verse
Of some old time not worth remembering,
And all the lovelier because a bubble.
Begin, begin, of some old king and queen,
Of Lugaid Redstripe or another; no, not him,
He and his lady perished wretchedly.

First Musician [*singing*]

'Why is it', Queen Edain said,
  'If I do but climb the stair . . .

Fergus. Ah! that is better. . . . They are alighted now.
Shake all your cockscombs, children; these are lovers.

[*Fergus goes out.*

First Musician

'Why is it', Queen Edain said,
  'If I do but climb the stair
To the tower overhead,
  When the winds are calling there,
Or the gannets calling out
  In waste places of the sky,
There's so much to think about
  That I cry, that I cry?'

Second Musician

But her goodman answered her:
  'Love would be a thing of naught
Had not all his limbs a stir
  Born out of immoderate thought;
Were he anything by half,
  Were his measure running dry.
Lovers, if they may not laugh,
  Have to cry, have to cry.'

[*Deirdre, Naoise, and Fergus have been seen for a moment
through the windows, but now they have entered.*

The Three Musicians [*together*]

But is Edain worth a song
  Now the hunt begins anew?
Praise the beautiful and strong;
  Praise the redness of the yew;

Praise the blossoming apple-stem.
But our silence had been wise.
What is all our praise to them
That have one another's eyes?

Deirdre. Silence your music, though I thank you for it;
But the wind's blown upon my hair, and I
Must set the jewels on my neck and head
For one that's coming.

Naoise.   Your colour has all gone
As 'twere with fear, and there's no cause for that.

Deirdre. These women have the raddle that they use
To make them brave and confident, although
Dread, toil, or cold may chill the blood o' their
          cheeks.
You'll help me, women. It is my husband's will
I show my trust in one that may be here
Before the mind can call the colour up.
My husband took these rubies from a king
Of Surracha that was so murderous
He seemed all glittering dragon. Now wearing them
Myself wars on myself, for I myself—
That do my husband's will, yet fear to do it—
Grow dragonish to myself.

> [*The women have gathered about her. Naoise has stood
> looking at her, but Fergus brings him to the chess-table.*

Naoise.   No messenger!
It's strange that there is none to welcome us.

Fergus. King Conchubar has sent no messenger
That he may come himself.

Naoise.   And being himself,

Being High King, he cannot break his faith.
I have his word and I must take that word,
Or prove myself unworthy of my nurture
Under a great man's roof.

Fergus.   We'll play at chess
Till the King comes. It is but natural
That she should doubt him, for her house has been
The hole of the badger and the den of the fox.

Naoise. If I had not King Conchubar's word I'd think
That chess-board ominous.

Fergus.   How can a board
That has been lying there these many years
Be lucky or unlucky?

Naoise.   It is the board
Where Lugaid Redstripe and that wife of his,
Who had a seamew's body half the year,
Played at the chess upon the night they died.

Fergus. I can remember now, a tale of treachery,
A broken promise and a journey's end—
But it were best forgot.
          [*Deirdre has been standing with the women about her.
          They have been helping her to put on her jewels and to
          put the pigment on her cheeks and arrange her hair.
          She has gradually grown attentive to what Fergus is
          saying.*

Naoise.   If the tale's true,
When it was plain that they had been betrayed,
They moved the men and waited for the end
As it were bedtime, and had so quiet minds

They hardly winked their eyes when the sword
    flashed.

Fergus. She never could have played so, being a woman,
    If she had not the cold sea's blood in her.

Deirdre. The gods turn clouds and casual accidents
    Into omens.

Naoise.   It would but ill become us,
    Now that King Conchubar has pledged his word,
    Should we be startled by a cloud or a shadow.

Deirdre. There's none to welcome us.

Naoise.   Being his guest,
    Words that would wrong him can but wrong our-
    selves.

Deirdre. An empty house upon the journey's end!
    Is that the way a king that means no mischief
    Honours a guest?

Fergus.   He is but making ready
    A welcome in his house, arranging where
    The moorhen and the mallard go, and where
    The speckled heathcock on a golden dish.

Deirdre. Had he no messenger?

Naoise.   Such words and fears
    Wrong this old man who's pledged his word to us.
    We must not speak or think as women do,
    That when the house is all a-bed sit up
    Marking among the ashes with a stick
    Till they are terrified.—Being what we are
    We must meet all things with an equal mind.
    [*To Fergus.*] Come, let us look if there's a messenger
    From Conchubar. We cannot see from this

Because we are blinded by the leaves and twigs,
But it may be the wood will thin again.
It is but kind that when the lips we love
Speak words that are unfitting for kings' ears
Our ears be deaf.

Fergus.   But now I had to threaten
These wanderers because they would have weighed
Some crazy phantasy of their own brain
Or gossip of the road with Conchubar's word.
If I had thought so little of mankind
I never could have moved him to this pardon.
I have believed the best of every man,
And find that to believe it is enough
To make a bad man show him at his best,
Or even a good man swing his lantern higher.
  [*Naoise and Fergus go out. The last words are spoken as
     they go through the door. One can see them through
     part of what follows, either through door or window.
     They move about, talking or looking along the road
     towards Conchubar's house.*

First Musician. If anything lies heavy on your heart,
Speak freely of it, knowing it is certain
That you will never see my face again.

Deirdre. You've been in love?

First Musician.   If you would speak of love,
Speak freely. There is nothing in the world
That has been friendly to us but the kisses
That were upon our lips, and when we are old
Their memory will be all the life we have.

Deirdre. There was a man that loved me. He was old;
I could not love him. Now I can but fear.

I

He has made promises, and brought me home;
But though I turn it over in my thoughts,
I cannot tell if they are sound and wholesome,
Or hackles on the hook.

First Musician.   I have heard he loved you
As some old miser loves the dragon-stone
He hides among the cobwebs near the roof.

Deirdre. You mean that when a man who has loved like
        that
Is after crossed, love drowns in its own flood,
And that love drowned and floating is but hate;
And that a king who hates sleeps ill at night
Till he has killed; and that, though the day laughs,
We shall be dead at cock-crow.

First Musician.   You've not my thought.
When I lost one I loved distractedly,
I blamed my crafty rival and not him,
And fancied, till my passion had run out,
That could I carry him away with me,
And tell him all my love, I'd keep him yet.

Deirdre. Ah! now I catch your meaning, that this king
Will murder Naoise, and keep me alive.

First Musician. 'Tis you that put that meaning upon
        words
Spoken at random.

Deirdre.   Wanderers like you,
Who have their wit alone to keep their lives,
Speak nothing that is bitter to the ear
At random; if they hint at it at all
Their eyes and ears have gathered it so lately
That it is crying out in them for speech.

First Musician. We have little that is certain.

Deirdre.   Certain or not,
  Speak it out quickly, I beseech you to it;
  I never have met any of your kind
  But that I gave them money, food, and fire.

First Musician. There are strange, miracle - working,
              wicked stones,
  Men tear out of the heart and the hot brain
  Of Libyan dragons.

Deirdre.   The hot Istain stone,
  And the cold stone of Fanes, that have power
  To stir even those at enmity to love.

First Musician. They have so great an influence, if but
              sewn
  In the embroideries that curtain in
  The bridal bed.

Deirdre.   O Mover of the stars
  That made this delicate house of ivory,
  And made my soul its mistress, keep it safe!

First Musician. I have seen a bridal bed, so curtained in,
  So decked for miracle in Conchubar's house,
  And learned that a bride's coming.

Deirdre.   And I the bride?
  Here is worse treachery than the seamew suffered,
  For she but died and mixed into the dust
  Of her dear comrade, but I am to live
  And lie in the one bed with him I hate.
  Where is Naoise? I was not alone like this
  When Conchubar first chose me for his wife;
  I cried in sleeping or waking and he came,
  But now there is worse need.

Naoise [*entering with Fergus*].   Why have you called?
  I was but standing there, without the door.

Deirdre. I have heard terrible mysterious things,
  Magical horrors and the spells of wizards.

Fergus. Why, that's no wonder. You have been listening
  To singers of the roads that gather up
  The stories of the world.

Deirdre.   But I have one
  To make the stories of the world but nothing.

Naoise. Be silent if it is against the King
  Whose guest you are.

Fergus.   No, let her speak it out.
  I know the High King's heart as it were my own,
  And can refute a slander, but already
  I have warned these women that it may be death.

Naoise. I will not weigh the gossip of the roads
  With the King's word. I ask your pardon for her:
  She has the heart of the wild birds that fear
  The net of the fowler or the wicker cage.

Deirdre. Am I to see the fowler and the cage
  And speak no word at all?

Naoise.   You would have known,
  Had they not bred you in that mountainous place,
  That when we give a word and take a word
  Sorrow is put away, past wrong forgotten.

Deirdre. Though death may come of it?

Naoise.   Though death may come.

Deirdre. When first we came into this empty house
  You had foreknowledge of our death, and even

When speaking of the paleness of my cheek
Your own cheek blanched.

Naoise.   Listen to this old man.
He can remember all the promises
We trusted to.

Deirdre.   You speak from the lips out,
And I am pleading for your life and mine.

Naoise. Listen to this old man, for many think
He has a golden tongue.

Deirdre.   Then I will say
What it were best to carry to the grave.
Look at my face where the leaf raddled it
And at these rubies on my hair and breast.
It was for him, to stir him to desire,
I put on beauty; yes, for Conchubar.

Naoise. What frenzy put these words into your mouth?

Deirdre. No frenzy, for what need is there for frenzy
To change what shifts with every change of the wind,
Or else there is no truth in men's old sayings?
Was I not born a woman?

Naoise.   You're mocking me.

Deirdre. And is there mockery in this face and eyes,
Or in this body, in these limbs that brought
So many mischiefs? Look at me and say
If that that shakes my limbs be mockery.

Naoise. What woman is there that a man can trust
But at the moment when he kisses her
At the first midnight?

Deirdre.   Were it not most strange
That women should put evil in men's hearts

And lack it in themselves? And yet I think
That being half good I might change round again
Were we aboard our ship and on the sea.

Naoise. We'll to the horses and take ship again.

Fergus. Fool, she but seeks to rouse your jealousy
　With crafty words.

Deirdre.　　　　　　Were we not born to wander?
　These jewels have been reaped by the innocent
　　　sword
　Upon a mountain, and a mountain bred me;
　But who can tell what change can come to love
　Among the valleys? I speak no falsehood now.
　Away to windy summits, and there mock
　The night-jar and the valley-keeping bird!

Fergus. Men blamed you that you stirred a quarrel up
　That has brought death to many. I have made peace,
　Poured water on the fire, but if you fly
　King Conchubar may think that he is mocked
　And the house blaze again: and in what quarter,
　If Conchubar were the treacherous man you think,
　Would you find safety now that you have come
　Into the very middle of his power,
　Under his very eyes?

Deirdre.　　　　　　Under his eyes
　And in the very middle of his power!
　Then there is but one way to make all safe,
　I'll spoil this beauty that brought misery
　And houseless wandering on the man I loved.
　These wanderers will show me how to do it;
　To clip this hair to baldness, blacken my skin
　With walnut juice, and tear my face with briars.

O that the creatures of the woods had torn
My body with their claws!

Fergus.   What, wilder yet!

Deirdre [*to Naoise*]. Whatever were to happen to my
    face
  I'd be myself, and there's not any way
  But this to bring all trouble to an end.

Naoise. Leave the gods' handiwork unblotched, and
    wait
  For their decision, our decision is past.

              [*A Dark-faced Messenger comes to the threshold.*

Fergus. Peace, peace; the messenger is at the door;
  He stands upon the threshold; he stands there;
  He stands, King Conchubar's purpose on his lips.

Messenger. Supper is on the table. Conchubar
  Is waiting for his guests.

Fergus.   All's well again!
  All's well! all's well! You cried your doubts so loud
  That I had almost doubted.

Naoise.   We doubted him,
  And he the while but busy in his house
  For the more welcome.

Deirdre.   The message is not finished.

Fergus. Come quickly. Conchubar will laugh, that I——
  Although I held out boldly in my speech—
  That I, even I——

Deirdre.   Wait, wait! He is not done.

Messenger. Deirdre and Fergus, son of Roigh, are
    summoned;
  But not the traitor that bore off the Queen.

It is enough that the King pardon her,
And call her to his table and his bed.

Naoise. So, then, it's treachery.

Fergus.   I'll not believe it.

Naoise. Lead on and I will follow at your heels
That I may challenge him before his court
To match me there, or match me in some place
Where none can come between us but our swords,
For I have found no truth on any tongue
That's not of iron.

Messenger.   I am Conchubar's man,
I am content to serve an iron tongue:
That Tongue commands that Fergus, son of Roigh,
And Deirdre come this night into his house,
And none but they.   [*He goes, followed by Naoise.*

Fergus.   Some rogue, some enemy,
Has bribed him to embroil us with the King;
I know that he has lied because I know
King Conchubar's mind as if it were my own,
But I'll find out the truth.
        [*He is about to follow Naoise, but Deirdre stops him.*

Deirdre.   No, no, old man.
You thought the best, and the worst came of it;
We listened to the counsel of the wise,
And so turned fools. But ride and bring your friends.
Go, and go quickly. Conchubar has not seen me;
It may be that his passion is asleep,
And that we may escape.

Fergus.   But I'll go first,
And follow up that Libyan heel, and send
Such words to Conchubar that he may know

At how great peril he lays hands upon you.

Naoise enters

Naoise. The Libyan, knowing that a servant's life
Is safe from hands like mine, but turned and mocked.

Fergus. I'll call my friends, and call the reaping-hooks.
And carry you in safety to the ships.
My name has still some power. I will protect,
Or, if that is impossible, revenge.
                    [*Goes out by other door.*

Naoise [*who is calm, like a man who has passed beyond life*].
The crib has fallen and the birds are in it;
There is not one of the great oaks about us
But shades a hundred men.

Deirdre.   Let's out and die,
Or break away, if the chance favour us.

Naoise. They would but drag you from me, stained
        with blood.
Their barbarous weapons would but mar that beauty,
And I would have you die as a queen should—
In a death-chamber. You are in my charge.
We will wait here, and when they come upon us,
I'll hold them from the doors, and when that's over,
Give you a cleanly death with this grey edge.

Deirdre. I will stay here; but you go out and fight.
Our way of life has brought no friends to us,
And if we do not buy them leaving it,
We shall be ever friendless.

Naoise.   What do they say?
That Lugaid Redstripe and that wife of his
Sat at this chess-board, waiting for their end.

They knew that there was nothing that could save
    them,
And so played chess as they had any night
For years, and waited for the stroke of sword.
I never heard a death so out of reach
Of common hearts, a high and comely end.
What need have I, that gave up all for love,
To die like an old king out of a fable,
Fighting and passionate? What need is there
For all that ostentation at my setting?
I have loved truly and betrayed no man.
I need no lightning at the end, no beating
In a vain fury at the cage's door.
[*To Musicians.*] Had you been here when that man
    and his queen
Played at so high a game, could you have found
An ancient poem for the praise of it?
It should have set out plainly that those two,
Because no man and woman have loved better,
Might sit on there contentedly, and weigh
The joy comes after. I have heard the seamew
Sat there, with all the colour in her cheeks,
As though she'd say: 'There's nothing happening
But that a king and queen are playing chess.'

Deirdre. He's in the right, though I have not been born
Of the cold, haughty waves, my veins being hot,
And though I have loved better than that queen,
I'll have as quiet fingers on the board.
O, singing women, set it down in a book,
That love is all we need, even though it is
But the last drops we gather up like this;
And though the drops are all we have known of life,

For we have been most friendless—praise us for it,
And praise the double sunset, for naught's lacking
But a good end to the long, cloudy day.

Naoise. Light torches there and drive the shadows out,
For day's grey end comes up.
        [*A Musician lights a torch in the fire and then crosses
        before the chess-players, and slowly lights the torches in
        the sconces. The light is almost gone from the wood,
        but there is a clear evening light in the sky, increasing
        the sense of solitude and loneliness.*

Deirdre.   Make no sad music.
    What is it but a king and queen at chess?
    They need a music that can mix itself
    Into imagination, but not break
    The steady thinking that the hard game needs.

        [*During the chess, the Musicians sing this song*]
            Love is an immoderate thing
                And can never be content
            Till it dip an ageing wing
                Where some laughing element
            Leaps and Time's old lanthorn dims.
                What's the merit in love-play,
            In the tumult of the limbs
                That dies out before 'tis day,
            Heart on heart, or mouth on mouth,
                All that mingling of our breath,
            When love-longing is but drouth
                For the things come after death?

        [*During the last verses Deirdre rises from the board and
        kneels at Naoise's feet.*

Deirdre. I cannot go on playing like that woman

That had but the cold blood of the sea in her veins.

Naoise. It is your move. Take up your man again.

Deirdre. Do you remember that first night in the woods
We lay all night on leaves, and looking up,
When the first grey of the dawn awoke the birds,
Saw leaves above us? You thought that I still slept,
And bending down to kiss me on the eyes,
Found they were open. Bend and kiss me now,
For it may be the last before our death.
And when that's over, we'll be different;
Imperishable things, a cloud or a fire.
And I know nothing but this body, nothing
But that old vehement, bewildering kiss.

> [*Conchubar comes to the door.*

First Musician. Children, beware!

Naoise [*laughing*]. He has taken up my challenge;
Whether I am a ghost or living man
When day has broken, I'll forget the rest,
And say that there is kingly stuff in him.

> [*Turns to fetch spear and shield, and then sees that
> Conchubar has gone.*

First Musician. He came to spy upon you, not to fight.

Naoise. A prudent hunter, therefore, but no king.
He'd find if what has fallen in the pit
Were worth the hunting, but has come too near,
And I turn hunter. You're not man, but beast.
Go scurry in the bushes, now, beast, beast,
For now it's topsy-turvy. I upon you.

> [*He rushes out after Conchubar.*

Deirdre. You have a knife there, thrust into your
girdle.

I'd have you give it me.

First Musician.   No, but I dare not.

Deirdre. No, but you must.

First Musician.   If harm should come to you,
  They'd know I gave it.

Deirdre [*snatching knife*].   There is no mark on this
  To make it different from any other
  Out of a common forge.
                              [*Goes to the door and looks out.*

First Musician.   You have taken it,
  I did not give it you; but there are times
  When such a thing is all the friend one has.

Deirdre. The leaves hide all, and there's no way to find
  What path to follow. Why is there no sound?
                              [*She goes from door to window.*

First Musician. Where would you go?

Deirdre.   To strike a blow for Naoise,
  If Conchubar call the Libyans to his aid.
  But why is there no clash? They have met by this!

First Musician. Listen. I am called wise. If Conchubar
        win,
  You have a woman's wile that can do much,
  Even with men in pride of victory.
  He is in love and old. What were one knife
  Among a hundred?

Deirdre [*going towards them*]. Women, if I die,
  If Naoise die this night, how will you praise?
  What words seek out? for that will stand to you;
  For being but dead we shall have many friends.
  All through your wanderings, the doors of kings
  Shall be thrown wider open, the poor man's hearth

Heaped with new turf, because you are wearing this
                                        [*Gives Musician a bracelet.*
To show that you have Deirdre's story right.

First Musician. Have you not been paid servants in love's
      house
   To sweep the ashes out and keep the doors?
   And though you have suffered all for mere love's
      sake
   You'd live your lives again.

Deirdre.   Even this last hour.

            Conchubar enters with dark-faced men

Conchubar. One woman and two men; that is the
      quarrel
   That knows no mending. Bring in the man she chose
   Because of his beauty and the strength of his youth.
      [*The dark-faced men drag in Naoise entangled in a net.*

Naoise. I have been taken like a bird or a fish.

Conchubar. He cried 'Beast, beast!' and in a blind-
      beast rage
   He ran at me and fell into the nets,
   But we were careful for your sake, and took him
   With all the comeliness that woke desire
   Unbroken in him. I being old and lenient,
   I would not hurt a hair upon his head.

Deirdre. What do you say? Have you forgiven him?

Naoise. He is but mocking us. What's left to say
   Now that the seven years' hunt is at an end?

Deirdre. He never doubted you until I made him,
   And therefore all the blame for what he says
   Should fall on me.

Conchubar.   But his young blood is hot,
And if we're of one mind, he shall go free,
And I ask nothing for it, or, if something,
Nothing I could not take. There is no king
In the wide world that, being so greatly wronged,
Could copy me, and give all vengeance up.
Although her marriage-day had all but come,
You carried her away; but I'll show mercy.
Because you had the insolent strength of youth
You carried her away; but I've had time
To think it out through all these seven years.
I will show mercy.

Naoise.   You have many words.

Conchubar. I will not make a bargain; I but ask
What is already mine.
    [*Deirdre moves slowly towards Conchubar while he is
    speaking, her eyes fixed upon him.*
                              You may go free
If Deirdre will but walk into my house
Before the people's eyes, that they may know,
When I have put the crown upon her head,
I have not taken her by force and guile.
The doors are open, and the floors are strewed
And in the bridal chamber curtains sewn
With all enchantments that give happiness
By races that are germane to the sun,
And nearest him, and have no blood in their veins—
For when they're wounded the wound drips with
      wine—
Nor speech but singing. At the bridal door
Two fair king's daughters carry in their hands
The crown and robe.

Deirdre.   O no! Not that, not that!
  Ask any other thing but that one thing.
  Leave me with Naoise. We will go away
  Into some country at the ends of the earth.
  We'll trouble you no more; and there is no one
  That will not praise you if you pardon us.
  'He is good, he is good', they'll say to one another;
  'There's nobody like him, for he forgave
  Deirdre and Naoise.'

Conchubar.   Do you think that I
  Shall let you go again, after seven years
  Of longing and of planning here and there,
  And trafficking with merchants for the stones
  That make all sure, and watching my own face
  That none might read it?

Deirdre [*to Naoise*].   It's better to go with him.
  Why should you die when one can bear it all?
  My life is over; it's better to obey.
  Why should you die? I will not live long, Naoise.
  I'd not have you believe I'd long stay living;
  O no, no, no! You will go far away.
  You will forget me. Speak, speak, Naoise, speak,
  And say that it is better that I go.
  I will not ask it. Do not speak a word,
  For I will take it all upon myself.
  Conchubar, I will go.

Naoise.   And do you think
  That, were I given life at such a price,
  I would not cast it from me? O my eagle!
  Why do you beat vain wings upon the rock
  When hollow night's above?

Deirdre.   It's better, Naoise.
   It may be hard for you, but you'll forget.
   For what am I, to be remembered always?
   And there are other women. There was one,
   The daughter of the King of Leodas;
   I could not sleep because of her. Speak to him;
   Tell it out plain, and make him understand.
   And if it be he thinks I shall stay living,
   Say that I will not.

Naoise.   Would I had lost life
   Among those Scottish kings that sought it of me
   Because you were my wife, or that the worst
   Had taken you before this bargaining!
   O eagle! If you were to do this thing,
   And buy my life of Conchubar with your body,
   Love's law being broken, I would stand alone
   Upon the eternal summits, and call out,
   And you could never come there, being banished.

Deirdre [*kneeling to Conchubar*]. I would obey, but cannot.
        Pardon us.
   I know that you are good. I have heard you praised
   For giving gifts; and you will pardon us,
   Although I cannot go into your house.
   It was my fault. I only should be punished.
                [Unseen by Deirdre, Naoise is gagged.
   The very moment these eyes fell on him,
   I told him; I held out my hands to him;
   How could he refuse? At first he would not—
   I am not lying—he remembered you.
   What do I say? My hands?—No, no, my lips—
   For I had pressed my lips upon his lips—

                                        K

I swear it is not false—my breast to his;

> [*Conchubar motions; Naoise, unseen by Deirdre, is taken behind the curtain.*

Until I woke the passion that's in all,
And how could he resist? I had my beauty.
You may have need of him, a brave, strong man,
Who is not foolish at the council-board,
Nor does he quarrel by the candle-light
And give hard blows to dogs. A cup of wine
Moves him to mirth, not madness.

> [*She stands up.*

What am I saying?
You may have need of him, for you have none
Who is so good a sword, or so well loved
Among the common people. You may need him,
And what king knows when the hour of need may
    come?
You dream that you have men enough. You laugh.
Yes; you are laughing to yourself. You say,
'I am Conchubar—I have no need of him.'
You will cry out for him some day and say,
'If Naoise were but living'——[*she misses Naoise*].
    Where is he?
Where have you sent him? Where is the son of
    Usna?
Where is he, O, where is he?

> [*She staggers over to the Musicians. The Executioner has come out with a sword on which there is blood; Conchubar points to it. The Musicians give a wail.*

Conchubar. The traitor who has carried off my wife
No longer lives. Come to my house now, Deirdre,
For he that called himself your husband's dead.

Deirdre. O, do not touch me. Let me go to him.

[*Pause.*

King Conchubar is right. My husband's dead.
A single woman is of no account,
Lacking array of servants, linen cupboards,
The bacon hanging—and King Conchubar's house
All ready, too—I'll to King Conchubar's house.
It is but wisdom to do willingly
What has to be.

Conchubar.   But why are you so calm?
I thought that you would curse me and cry out,
And fall upon the ground and tear your hair.

Deirdre [*laughing*]. You know too much of women to
          think so;
Though, if I were less worthy of desire,
I would pretend as much; but, being myself,
It is enough that you were master here.
Although we are so delicately made,
There's something brutal in us, and we are won
By those who can shed blood. It was some woman
That taught you how to woo: but do not touch
          me:
I shall do all you bid me, but not yet,
Because I have to do what's customary.
We lay the dead out, folding up the hands,
Closing the eyes, and stretching out the feet,
And push a pillow underneath the head,
Till all's in order; and all this I'll do
For Naoise, son of Usna.

Conchubar.   It is not fitting.
You are not now a wanderer, but a queen,
And there are plenty that can do these things.

Deirdre [*motioning Conchubar away*]. No, no. Not yet.
    cannot be your queen
  Till the past's finished, and its debts are paid.
  When a man dies, and there are debts unpaid,
  He wanders by the debtor's bed and cries,
  'There's so much owing.'

Conchubar.   You are deceiving me.
  You long to look upon his face again.
  Why should I give you now to a dead man
  That took you from a living?
                          [*He makes a step towards her.*
Deirdre.   In good time.
  You'll stir me to more passion than he could,
  And yet, if you are wise, you'll grant me this:
  That I go look upon him that was once
  So strong and comely and held his head so high
  That women envied me. For I will see him
  All blood-bedabbled and his beauty gone.
  It's better, when you're beside me in your strength,
  That the mind's eye should call up the soiled body,
  And not the shape I loved. Look at him, women.
  He heard me pleading to be given up,
  Although my lover was still living, and yet
  He doubts my purpose. I will have you tell him
  How changeable all women are; how soon
  Even the best of lovers is forgot
  When his day's finished.

Conchubar.   No; but I will trust
  The strength that you have praised, and not your
    purpose.

Deirdre [*almost with a caress*]. It is so small a gift and you
  will grant it

Because it is the first that I have asked.
He has refused. There is no sap in him;
Nothing but empty veins. I thought as much.
He has refused me the first thing I have asked—
Me, me, his wife. I understand him now;
I know the sort of life I'll have with him;
But he must drag me to his house by force.
If he refuses [*she laughs*], he shall be mocked of all.
They'll say to one another, 'Look at him
That is so jealous that he lured a man
From over sea, and murdered him, and yet
He trembled at the thought of a dead face!'
                              [*She has her hand upon the curtain.*

Conchubar. How do I know that you have not some
    knife,
    And go to die upon his body?

Deirdre.   Have me searched,
    If you would make so little of your queen.
    It may be that I have a knife hid here
    Under my dress. Bid one of these dark slaves
    To search me for it.   [*Pause.*

Conchubar.   Go to your farewells, Queen.

Deirdre. Now strike the wire, and sing to it a while,
    Knowing that all is happy, and that you know
    Within what bride-bed I shall lie this night,
    And by what man, and lie close up to him,
    For the bed's narrow, and there outsleep the cock-
    crow.   [*She goes behind the curtain.*

First Musician. They are gone, they are gone. The proud
    may lie by the proud.

Second Musician. Though we were bidden to sing, cry
    nothing loud.

First Musician. They are gone, they are gone.

Second Musician.   Whispering were enough.

First Musician. Into the secret wilderness of their love.

Second Musician. A high, grey cairn. What more is to
    be said?

First Musician. Eagles have gone into their cloudy bed.
    [*Shouting outside. Fergus enters. Many men with scythes
    and sickles and torches gather about the doors. The
    house is lit with the glare of their torches.*

Fergus. Where's Naoise, son of Usna, and his queen?
    I and a thousand reaping-hooks and scythes
    Demand him of you.

Conchubar.   You have come too late.
    I have accomplished all. Deirdre is mine;
    She is my queen, and no man now can rob me.
    I had to climb the topmost bough, and pull
    This apple among the winds. Open the curtain
    That Fergus learn my triumph from her lips.
    [*The curtain is drawn back. The Musicians begin to keen
    with low voices.*
    No, no; I'll not believe it. She is not dead—
    She cannot have escaped a second time!

Fergus. King, she is dead; but lay no hand upon her.
    What's this but empty cage and tangled wire,
    Now the bird's gone? But I'll not have you touch it.

Conchubar. You are all traitors, all against me—all.
    And she has deceived me for a second time;
    And every common man can keep his wife,

But not the King.

[*Loud shouting outside*: 'Death to Conchubar!' 'Where
is Naoise?' etc. *The dark-faced men gather round
Conchubar and draw their swords; but he motions
them away.*

     I have no need of weapons,
There's not a traitor that dare stop my way.
Howl, if you will; but I, being King, did right
In choosing her most fitting to be Queen,
And letting no boy lover take the sway.

THE END

THE GREEN HELMET

An Heroic Farce

1910

THE GREEN HELMET

An Heroic Farce

PERSONS IN THE PLAY

Laegaire	Laegaire's Wife
Conall	Conall's Wife
Cuchulain	Laeg, *Cuchulain's chariot-driver*
Red Man, *a Spirit*	Stable Boys and Scullions
Emer	Black Men, etc.

A house made of logs. There are two windows at the back and a door which cuts off one of the corners of the room. Through the door one can see low rocks which make the ground outside higher than it is within, and beyond the rocks a misty moon-lit sea. Through the windows one can see nothing but the sea. There is a great chair at the opposite side to the door, and in front of it a table with cups and a flagon of ale. Here and there are stools.

At the Abbey Theatre the house is orange red and the chairs and tables and flagons black, with a slight purple tinge which is not clearly distinguishable from the black. The rocks are black with a few green touches. The sea is green and luminous, and all the characters except the Red Man and the Black Men are dressed in various shades of green, one or two with touches of purple which look nearly black. The Black Men all wear dark purple and have eared caps, and at the end their eyes should look green from the reflected light of the sea. The Red Man is altogether in red. He is very tall, and his height increased by horns on the Green Helmet. The effect is intentionally violent and startling.

Laegaire. What is that? I had thought that I saw, though
     but in the wink of an eye,
   A cat-headed man out of Connacht go pacing and
     spitting by;
   But that could not be.

Conall. You have dreamed it—there's nothing out there
   I killed them all before daybreak—I hoked them out
     of their lair;
   I cut off a hundred heads with a single stroke of my
     sword,
   And then I danced on their graves and carried away
     their hoard.

Laegaire. Does anything stir on the sea?

Conall.   Not even a fish or a gull:
   I can see for a mile or two, now that the moon's at
     the full.   [*A distant shout.*

Laegaire. Ah—there—there is some one who calls us.

Conall.   But from the landward side,
   And we have nothing to fear that has not come up
     from the tide;
   The rocks and the bushes cover whoever made that
     noise,
   But the land will do us no harm.

Laegaire.   It was like Cuchulain's voice.

Conall. But that's an impossible thing.

Laegaire.   An impossible thing indeed.

Conall. For he will never come home, he has all that
     he could need
   In that high windy Scotland—good luck in all that he
     does.

Here neighbour wars on neighbour, and why there
　is no man knows,
And if a man is lucky all wish his luck away,
And take his good name from him between a day
　and a day.

Laegaire. I would he'd come for all that, and make his
　young wife know
　That though she may be his wife, she has no right
　　to go
　Before your wife and my wife, as she would have
　　done last night
　Had they not caught at her dress, and pulled her as
　　was right;
　And she makes light of us though our wives do all
　　that they can.
　She spreads her tail like a peacock and praises none
　　but her man.

Conall. A man in a long green cloak that covers him
　up to the chin
　Comes down through the rocks and hazels.

Laegaire. 　　　　Cry out that he cannot come in.

Conall. He must look for his dinner elsewhere, for no
　one alive shall stop
　Where a shame must alight on us two before the
　　dawn is up.

Laegaire. No man on the ridge of the world must ever
　know that but us two.

Conall [*outside door*]. Go away, go away, go away.

Young Man [*outside door*]. I will go when the night is
　through

And I have eaten and slept and drunk to my heart's
    delight.

Conall. A law has been made that none shall sleep in
    this house to-night.

Young Man. Who made that law?

Conall.   We made it, and who has so good a right?
    Who else has to keep the house from the Shape-
    Changers till day?

Young Man. Then I will unmake the law, so get you
    out of the way.

                 [*He pushes past Conall and goes into house.*

Conall. I thought no living man could have pushed me
    from the door,
    Nor could any living man do it but for the dip in
    the floor;
    And had I been rightly ready there's no man living
    could do it,
    Dip or no dip.

Laegaire.   Go out—if you have your wits, go out,
    A stone's throw further on you will find a big house
    where
    Our wives will give you supper, and you'll sleep
    sounder there,
    For it's a luckier house.

Young Man.   I'll eat and sleep where I will.

Laegaire. Go out or I will make you.

Young Man [*forcing up Laegaire's arm, passing him and
    putting his shield on the wall over the chair*]. Not till
    I have drunk my fill,
    But may some dog defend me, for a cat of wonder's
    up.

Laegaire and Conall are here, the flagon full to the
    top,
And the cups—

Laegaire.   It is Cuchulain.

Cuchulain.   The cups are dry as a bone.
                          [He sits on chair and drinks.

Conall. Go into Scotland again, or where you will, but
    begone
From this unlucky country that was made when the
    Devil spat.

Cuchulain. If I lived here a hundred years, could a worse
    thing come than that
Laegaire and Conall should know me and bid me
    begone to my face?

Conall. We bid you begone from a house that has fallen
    on shame and disgrace.

Cuchulain. I am losing patience, Conall—I find you
    stuffed with pride,
The flagon full to the brim, the front door standing
    wide;
You'd put me off with words, but the whole thing's
    plain enough,
You are waiting for some message to bring you to
    war or love
In that old secret country beyond the wool-white
    waves,
Or it may be down beneath them in foam-be-
    wildered caves
Where nine forsaken sea-queens fling shuttles to and
    fro;

But beyond them, or beneath them, whether you will
   or no,
I am going too.

Laegaire.   Better tell it all out to the end;
  He was born to luck in the cradle, his good luck may
     amend
  The bad luck we were born to.

Conall.   I'll lay the whole thing bare.
  You saw the luck that he had when he pushed in
     past me there.
  Does anything stir on the sea?

Laegaire.   Not even a fish or a gull.

Conall. You were gone but a little while. We were
    there and the ale-cup full.
  We were half drunk and merry, and midnight on
    the stroke,
  When a wide, high man came in with a red foxy
    cloak,
  With half-shut foxy eyes and a great laughing mouth,
  And he said, when we bid him drink, that he had so
    great a drouth
  He could drink the sea.

Cuchulain.   I thought he had come for one of you
  Out of some Connacht rath, and would lap up
    milk and mew;
  But if he so loved water I have the tale awry.

Conall. You would not be so merry if he were standing
    by,
  For when we had sung or danced as he were our next
    of kin

He promised to show us a game, the best that ever
    had been;
And when we had asked what game, he answered,
    'Why, whip off my head!
Then one of you two stoop down, and I'll whip off
    his', he said.
'A head for a head', he said, 'that is the game that I
    play'.

Cuchulain. How could he whip off a head when his
    own had been whipped away?

Conall. We told him it over and over, and that ale had
    fuddled his wit,
But he stood and laughed at us there, as though his
    sides would split,
Till I could stand it no longer, and whipped off his
    head at a blow,
Being mad that he did not answer, and more at his
    laughing so,
And there on the ground where it fell it went on
    laughing at me.

Laegaire. Till he took it up in his hands—

Conall.   And splashed himself into the sea.

Cuchulain. I have imagined as good when I've been as
    deep in the cup.

Laegaire. You never did.

Cuchulain.   And believed it.

Conall.   Cuchulain, when will you stop
Boasting of your great deeds and weighing yourself
    with us two,
And crying out to the world, whatever we say or do,

That you've said or done a better?—Nor is it a
    drunkard's tale,
Though we said to ourselves at first that it all came
    out of the ale,
And thinking that if we told it we should be a
    laughing-stock
Swore we should keep it secret.

Laegaire.   But twelve months upon the clock—

Conall. A twelvemonth from the first time—

Laegaire.   And the jug full up to the brim:
For we had been put from our drinking by the very
    thought of him—

Conall. We stood as we're standing now—

Laegaire.   The horns were as empty—

Conall.   When
He ran up out of the sea with his head on his
    shoulders again.

Cuchulain. Why, this is a tale worth telling.

Conall.   And he called for his debt and his right,
And said that the land was disgraced because of us
    two from that night
If we did not pay him his debt.

Laegaire.   What is there to be said
When a man with a right to get it has come to ask
    for your head?

Conall. If you had been sitting there you had been
    silent like us.

Laegaire. He said that in twelve months more he would
    come again to this house
And ask his debt again. Twelve months are up to-day.

Conall. He would have followed after if we had run
away.

Laegaire. Will he tell every mother's son that we have
broken our word?

Cuchulain. Whether he does or does not, we'll drive
him out with the sword,
And take his life in the bargain if he but dare to
scoff.

Conall. How can you fight with a head that laughs
when you've whipped it off?

Laegaire. Or a man that can pick it up and carry it out
in his hand?

Conall. He is coming now, there's a splash and a
rumble along the strand
As when he came last.

Cuchulain.   Come, and put all your backs to the door.
[*A tall red-headed, red-cloaked man stands upon the
threshold against the misty green of the sea; the ground,
higher without than within the house, makes him seem
taller even than he is. He leans upon a great two-
handed sword.*

Laegaire. It is too late to shut it, for there he stands
once more
And laughs like the sea.

Cuchulain. Old herring—You whip off heads! Why,
then,
Whip off your own, for it seems you can clap it on
again.
Or else go down in the sea, go down in the sea, I say,
Find that old juggler Manannan and whip his head
away;

Or the Red Man of the Boyne, for they are of your
 own sort,
Or if the waves have vexed you and you would find a
 sport
Of a more Irish fashion, go fight without a rest
A caterwauling phantom among the winds of the
 West.
But what are you waiting for? Into the water, I say!
If there's no sword can harm you, I've an older trick
 to play,
An old five-fingered trick to tumble you out of the
 place;
I am Sualtim's son, Cuchulain—What, do you laugh
 in my face?

Red Man. So you too think me in earnest in wagering
 poll for poll!
A drinking joke and a gibe and a juggler's feat, that
 is all,
To make the time go quickly—for I am the drinker's
 friend,
The kindest of all Shape-Changers from here to the
 world's end,
The best of all tipsy companions. And now I bring
 you a gift:
I will lay it there on the ground for the best of you
 all to lift *[He lays his Helmet on the ground.*
And wear upon his own head, and choose for your-
 selves the best.
O, Laegaire and Conall are brave, but they were
 afraid of my jest.
Well, maybe I jest too grimly when the ale is in the
 cup.

There, I'm forgiven now—

       [*Then in a more solemn voice as he goes out.*

              Let the bravest take it up.

   [*Conall takes up Helmet and gazes at it with delight.*

Laegaire [*singing, with a swaggering stride*].

         Laegaire is best;

         Between water and hill,

         He fought in the West

         With cat-heads, until

         At the break of day

         All fell by his sword,

         And he carried away

         Their hidden hoard.

                  [*He seizes the Helmet.*

Conall. Laegaire, that Helmet is mine, for what did you
    find in the bag

  But the straw and the broken delf and the bits of
    dirty rag

  You'd taken for good money?

Cuchulain.   No, no, but give it me.

                     [*He takes Helmet.*

Conall. The Helmet's mine or Laegaire's—you're the
    youngest of us three.

Cuchulain [*filling Helmet with ale*]. I did not take it to
    keep it—the Red Man gave it for one,

  But I shall give it to all—to all of us three or to
    none;

  That is as you look upon it—we will pass it to and
    fro,

  And time and time about, drink out of it and so

  Stroke into peace this cat that has come to take our
    lives.

Now it is purring again, and now I drink to your
wives,
And I drink to Emer, my wife.

> [*A great noise without and shouting.*
Why, what in God's name is that noise?

Conall. What else but the charioteers and the kitchen
and stable boys
Shouting against each other, and the worst of all is
your own,
That chariot-driver, Laeg, and they'll keep it up till
the dawn,
And there's not a man in the house that will close
his eyes to-night,
Or be able to keep them from it, or know what set
them to fight.   [*A noise of horns without.*
There, do you hear them now? Such hatred has each
for each
They have taken the hunting-horns to drown one
another's speech
For fear the truth may prevail. -Here's your good
health and long life
And, though she be quarrelsome, good health to
Emer, your wife.

> [*The Charioteers, Stable Boys, and Scullions come run-
ning in. They carry great horns and other instruments,
ladles, and the like.*

Laeg. I am Laeg, Cuchulain's driver, and my master's
cock of the yard.

Another Charioteer. Conall would scatter his feathers.

> [*Confused murmurs.*

Laegaire [*to Cuchulain*]. No use, they won't hear a word.

Conall. They'll keep it up till the dawn.

Another Charioteer.   It is Laegaire that is the best,
  For he fought with cats in Connacht while Conall
    took his rest
  And drained his ale-pot.

Another.   Laegaire—what does a man of his sort
  Care for the like of us? He did it for his own sport.

Another. It was all mere luck at the best.

Another.   But Conall, I say—

Another.   Let me speak.

Laeg. You'd be dumb if the cock of the yard would
  but open his beak.

Another. Before your cock was born, my master was in
  the fight.

Laeg. Go home and praise your grand-dad. They took
  to the horns for spite,
  For I said that no cock of your sort had been born
  since the fight began.

Another. Conall has got it, the best man has got it, and
  I am his man.

Cuchulain. Who was it started this quarrel?

A Stable Boy.   It was Laeg.

Another.   It was Laeg done it all.

Laeg. A high, wide, foxy man came where we sat in
  the hall,
  Getting our supper ready, with a great voice like the
  wind,
  And cried that there was a helmet, or something of
  the kind,
  That was for the foremost man upon the ridge of the
  earth.

So I cried your name through the hall,

[*The others cry out and blow horns, partly drowning the rest of his speech.*

                         but they denied its worth,

Preferring Laegaire or Conall, and they cried to drown my voice;

But I have so strong a throat that I drowned all their noise

Till they took to the hunting-horns and blew them into my face,

And as neither side would give in—we would settle it in this place.

Let the Helmet be taken from Conall.

A Stable Boy.   No, Conall is the best man here.

Another. Give it to Laegaire that made the murderous cats pay dear.

Cuchulain. It has been given to none: that our rivalry might cease,

We have turned that murderous cat into a cup of peace.

I drank the first; and then Conall; give it to Laegaire now   [*Conall gives Helmet to Laegaire.*

That it may purr in his hand and all of our servants know

That, since the ale went in, its claws went out of sight.

A Servant. That's well—I will stop my shouting.

Another.   Cuchulain is in the right;

I am tired of this big horn that has made me hoarse as a rook.

Laegaire. Cuchulain, you drank the first.

Another.   By drinking the first he took
  The whole of the honours himself.

Laegaire.   Cuchulain, you drank the first.

Another. If Laegaire drink from it now, he claims to be
      last and worst.

Another. Cuchulain and Conall have drunk.

Another.   He is lost if he taste a drop.

Laegaire [*laying Helmet on table*]. Did you claim to be
      better than us by drinking first from the cup?

Cuchulain [*his words are partly drowned by the murmurs of
      the crowd though he speaks very loud*]. That juggler
      from the sea, that old red herring it is
  Who has set us all by the ears—he brought the
      Helmet for this,
  And because we would not quarrel he ran elsewhere
      to shout
  That Conall and Laegaire wronged me, till all had
      fallen out.
        [*The murmur grows less so that his words are heard.*
  Who knows where he is now or whom he is spurring
      to fight?
  So get you gone, and whatever may cry aloud in the
      night,
  Or show itself in the air, be silent until morn.

A Servant. Cuchulain is in the right—I am tired of this
      big horn.

Cuchulain. Go!
      [*The Servants turn towards the door but stop on hearing
      the voices of women outside.*

Laegaire's Wife [*without*]. Mine is the better to look at.

Conall's Wife [*without*].   But mine is better born.

Emer [*without*]. My man is the pithier man.

Cuchulain.   Old hurricane, well done!
   You've set our wives to the game that they may egg
      us on;
   We are to kill each other that you may sport with
      us.
   Ah, now they've begun to wrestle as to who'll be
      first in the house.
                 [*The women come to the door struggling.*

Emer. No, I have the right of place, for I married the
   better man.

Conall's Wife [*pulling Emer back*]. My nails in your neck
   and shoulder.

Laegaire's Wife.   And go before me if you can.
   My husband fought in the West.

Conall's Wife [*kneeling in the door so as to keep the others out*
     who pull at her]. But what did he fight with there
   But sidelong and spitting and helpless shadows of the
      dim air?
   And what did he carry away but straw and broken
      delf?

Laegaire's Wife. Your own man made up that tale
   trembling alone by himself,
   Drowning his terror.

Emer [*forcing herself in front*]. I am Emer, it is I go first
   through the door.
   No one shall walk before me, or praise any man
     before
   My man has been praised.

Cuchulain. [*putting his spear across the door so as to close it*].
                Come, put an end to their quarrelling:
One is as fair as the other, each one the wife of a
    king.
Break down the painted walls, break them down,
    down to the floor!
Our wives shall come in together, each one at her
    own door.
    [*Laegaire and Conall begin to break down the walls.
    Their wives go each to the hole her husband is making.
    Emer stands at the door and sings. Some of those who
    carry musical instruments may play an accompaniment.*

Emer.

                Nothing that he has done;
                His mind that is fire,
                His body that is sun,
                Have set my head higher
                Than all the world's wives.
                Himself on the wind
                Is the gift that he gives,
                Therefore women-kind,
                When their eyes have met mine,
                Grow cold and grow hot,
                Troubled as with wine
                By a secret thought,
                Preyed upon, fed upon
                By jealousy and desire,
                For I am moon to that sun,
                I am steel to that fire.

    [*Holes have been broken in the walls. Cuchulain takes his
    spear from the door, and the three women come in at the
    same moment.*

Emer.   Cuchulain, put off this sloth and awake:
  I will sing till I've stiffened your lip against every
      knave that would take
  A share of your honour.

Laegaire's Wife. You lie, for your man would take from
      my man.

Conall's Wife [*to Laegaire's Wife*]. You say that, you
      double-face, and your own husband began.

Cuchulain [*taking up Helmet from table*]. Townland may
      rail at townland till all have gone to wrack,
  The very straws may wrangle till they've thrown
      down the stack;
  The very door-posts bicker till they've pulled in the
      door,
  The very ale-jars jostle till the ale is on the floor,
  But this shall help no further.

                   [*He throws Helmet into the sea.*

Laegaire's Wife.   It was not for your head,
  And so you would let none wear it, but fling it away
      instead.

Conall's Wife. But you shall answer for it, for you've
      robbed my man by this.

Conall. You have robbed us both, Cuchulain.

Laegaire.   The greatest wrong there is
  On the wide ridge of the world has been done to
      us two this day.

Emer [*drawing her dagger.*] Who is for Cuchulain?

Cuchulain.   Silence.

Emer.   Who is for Cuchulain, I say?
    [*She sings the same words as before, flourishing her
      dagger about. While she is singing, Conall's Wife and*

*Laegaire's Wife draw their daggers and run at her,
but Cuchulain forces them back. Laegaire and Conall
draw their swords to strike Cuchulain.*

Laegaire's Wife [*crying out so as to be heard through Emer's
singing*]. Deafen her singing with horns!

Conall's Wife.   Cry aloud! blow horns! make a noise!

Laegaire's Wife. Blow horns, clap hands, or shout, so that
you smother her voice!
  [*The Stable Boys and Scullions blow their horns or fight
  among themselves. There is a deafening noise and a
  confused fight. Suddenly three black hands come through
  the windows and put out the torches. It is now pitch-
  dark, but for a faint light outside the house which
  merely shows that there are moving forms, but not who
  or what they are, and in the darkness one can hear low
  terrified voices.*

A Voice. Coal-black, and headed like cats, they came
up over the strand.

Another Voice. And I saw one stretch to a torch and
cover it with his hand.

Another Voice. Another sooty fellow has plucked the
moon from the air.
  [*A light gradually comes into the house from the sea, on
  which the moon begins to show once more. There is no
  light within the house, and the great beams of the walls
  are dark and full of shadows, and the persons of the
  play dark too against the light. The Red Man is seen
  standing in the midst of the house. The black cat-
  headed men crouch and stand about the door. One
  carries the Helmet, one the great sword.*

Red Man. I demand the debt that's owing. Let some man kneel down there
That I may cut his head off, or all shall go to wrack.

Cuchulain. He played and paid with his head, and it's right that we pay him back,
And give him more than he gave, for he comes in here as a guest:
So I will give him my head.   [*Emer begins to keen.*
                    Little wife, little wife, be at rest.
Alive I have been far off in all lands under the sun,
And been no faithful man; but when my story is done
My fame shall spring up and laugh, and set you high above all.

Emer [*putting her arms about him*]. It is you, not your fame that I love.

Cuchulain [*tries to put her from him*]. You are young, you are wise, you can call
Some kinder and comelier man that will sit at home in the house.

Emer. Live and be faithless still.

Cuchulain [*throwing her from him*]. Would you stay the great barnacle-goose
When its eyes are turned to the sea and its beak to the salt of the air?

Emer [*lifting her dagger to stab herself*]. I, too, on the grey wing's path!

Cuchulain [*seizing dagger*]. Do you dare, do you dare, do you dare?

Bear children and sweep the house.

    [Forcing his way through the servants who gather round.

               Wail, but keep from the road.

        [He kneels before Red Man. There is a pause.

Quick to your work, old Radish, you will fade when
    the cocks have crowed.

    *[A black cat-headed man holds out the Helmet. The Red
    Man takes it.*

Red Man. I have not come for your hurt, I'm the Rector
    of this land,

And with my spitting cat-heads, my frenzied moon-
    bred band,

Age after age I sift it, and choose for its champion-
    ship

The man who hits my fancy.

            [He places the Helmet on Cuchulain's head.

               And I choose the laughing lip

That shall not turn from laughing, whatever rise or
    fall;

The heart that grows no bitterer although betrayed
    by all;

The hand that loves to scatter; the life like a
    gambler's throw;

And these things I make prosper, till a day come that
    I know,

When heart and mind shall darken that the weak
    may end the strong,

And the long-remembering harpers have matter for
    their song.

THE END

THE SHADOWY WATERS

(Acting Version)

1911

M

THE SHADOWY WATERS

(Acting Version)

PERSONS IN THE PLAY

Forgael   Sailors

Aibric   Dectora

A mast and a great sail, a large tiller, a poop rising several feet above the stage, and from the overhanging stern a lanthorn hanging. The sea or sky is represented by a semicircular cloth of which nothing can be seen except a dark abyss. The persons move but little. Some sailors are discovered crouching by the sail. Forgael is asleep and Aibric standing by the tiller on the raised poop.

First Sailor. It is long enough, and too long, Forgael has been bringing us through the waste places of the great sea.

Second Sailor. We did not meet with a ship to make a prey of these eight weeks, or any shore or island to plunder or to harry. It is a hard thing, age to be coming on me, and I not to get the chance of doing a robbery that would enable me to live quiet and honest to the end of my lifetime.

First Sailor. We are out since the new moon. What is worse again, it is the way we are in a ship, the barrels empty and my throat shrivelled with drought, and nothing to quench it but water only.

Forgael [*in his sleep*]. Yes; there, there; that hair that is the colour of burning.

First Sailor. Listen to him now, calling out in his sleep.

Forgael [*in his sleep*]. That pale forehead, that hair the colour of burning.

First Sailor. Some crazy dream he is in, and believe me it is no crazier than the thought he has waking. He is not the first that has had the wits drawn out from him through shadows and fantasies.

Second Sailor. That is what ails him. I have been thinking it this good while.

First Sailor. Do you remember that galley we sank at the time of the full moon?

Second Sailor. I do. We were becalmed the same night, and he sat up there playing that old harp of his until the moon had set.

First Sailor. I was sleeping up there by the bulwark, and when I woke in the sound of the harp a change came over my eyes, and I could see very strange things. The dead were floating upon the sea yet, and it seemed as if the life that went out of every one of them had turned to the shape of a man-headed bird—grey they were, and they rose up of a sudden and called out with voices like our own, and flew away singing to the west. Words like this they were singing: 'Happiness beyond measure, happiness where the sun dies'.

Second Sailor. I understand well what they are doing. My mother used to be talking of birds of the sort. They are sent by the lasting watchers to lead men away from this world and its women to some place of shining women that cast no shadow, having lived before the making of the earth. But I have no mind to go following him to that place.

First Sailor. Let us creep up to him and kill him in his sleep.

Second Sailor. I would have made an end of him long ago, but that I was in dread of his harp. It is said that when he plays upon it he has power over all the listeners, with or without the body, seen or unseen, and any man that listens grows to be as mad as himself.

First Sailor. What way can he play it, being in his sleep?

Second Sailor. But who would be our captain then to make out a course from the Bear and the Polestar, and to bring us back home?

First Sailor. I have that thought out. We must have Aibric with us. He knows the constellations as well as Forgael. He is a good hand with the sword. Join with us; be our captain, Aibric. We are agreed to put an end to Forgael, before he wakes. There is no man but will be glad of it when it is done. Join with us, and you will have the captain's share and profit.

Aibric. Silence! for you have taken Forgael's pay.

First Sailor. Little pay we have had this twelvemonth. We would never have turned against him if he had brought us, as he promised, into seas that would be thick with ships. That was the bargain. What is the use of knocking about and fighting as we do unless we get the chance to drink more wine and kiss more women than lasting peaceable men through their long

lifetime? You will be as good a leader as ever he was
himself, if you will but join us.

Aibric. And do you think that I will join myself
To men like you, and murder him who has been
My master from my earliest childhood up?
No! nor to a world of men like you
When Forgael's in the other scale. Come! come!
I'll answer to more purpose when you have drawn
That sword out of its scabbard.

First Sailor.   You have awaked him.
We had best go, for we have missed this chance.

                                   [*Sailors go out.*

Forgael. Have the birds passed us? I could hear your
    voice,
But there were others.

Aibric.   I have seen nothing pass.

Forgael. You are certain of it? I never wake from sleep
But that I am afraid they may have passed;
For they're my only pilots. I have not seen them
For many days, and yet there must be many
Dying at every moment in the world.

Aibric. They have all but driven you crazy, and already
The sailors have been plotting for your death;
Whatever has been cried into your ears
Has lured you on to death.

Forgael.   No; but they promised—

Aibric. I know their promises. You have told me all.
They are to bring you to unheard-of passion,
To some strange love the world knows nothing of,
Some Ever-living woman as you think,
One that can cast no shadow, being unearthly.

But that's all folly. Turn the ship about,
Sail home again, be some fair woman's friend;
Be satisfied to live like other men,
And drive impossible dreams away. The world
Has beautiful women to please every man.

Forgael. But he that gets their love after the fashion
Loves in brief longing and deceiving hope
And bodily tenderness, and finds that even
The bed of love, that in the imagination
Had seemed to be the giver of all peace,
Is no more than a wine-cup in the tasting,
And as soon finished.

Aibric.   All that ever loved
Have loved that way—there is no other way.

Forgael. Yet never have two lovers kissed but they
Believed there was some other near at hand,
And almost wept because they could not find it.

Aibric. When they have twenty years; in middle life
They take a kiss for what a kiss is worth,
And let the dream go by.

Forgael.   It's not a dream,
But the reality that makes our passion
As a lamp shadow—no—no lamp, the sun.
What the world's million lips are thirsting for
Must be substantial somewhere.

Aibric.   I have heard the Druids
Mutter such things as they awake from trance.
It may be that the dead have lit upon it,
Or those that never lived; no mortal can.

Forgael. I only of all living men shall find it.

Aibric. Then seek it in the habitable world,

Or leap into that sea and end a journey
That has no other end.

Forgael.   I cannot answer.
I can see nothing plain; all's mystery.
Yet sometimes there's a torch inside my head
That makes all clear, but when the light is gone
I have but images, analogies,
The mystic bread, the sacramental wine,
The red rose where the two shafts of the cross,
Body and soul, waking and sleep, death, life,
Whatever meaning ancient allegorists
Have settled on, are mixed into one joy.
For what's the rose but that? miraculous cries,
Old stories about mystic marriages,
Impossible truths? But when the torch is lit
All that is impossible is certain,
I plunge in the abyss.   [*Sailors come in.*

First Sailor. Look there! there in the mist! A ship of spices!

Second Sailor. We would not have noticed her but for the sweet smell through the air. Ambergris and sandalwood, and all the herbs the witches bring from the sunrise.

First Sailor. No; but opoponax and cinnamon.

Forgael [*taking the tiller from Aibric*]. The Ever-living have kept my bargain; they have paid you on the nail.

Aibric. Take up that rope to make her fast while we are plundering her.

First Sailor. There is a king on her deck and a queen. Where there is one woman it is certain there will be others.

Aibric. Speak lower or they'll hear.

First Sailor. They cannot hear; they are too much taken up with one another. Look! he has stooped down and kissed her on the lips.

Second Sailor. When she finds out we have as good men aboard she may not be too sorry in the end.

First Sailor. She will be as dangerous as a wild cat. These queens think more of the riches and the great name they get by marriage than of a ready hand and a strong body.

Second Sailor. There is nobody is natural but a robber. That is the reason the whole world goes tottering about upon its bandy legs.

Aibric. Run upon them now, and overpower the crew while yet asleep.

> [*Sailors and Aibric go out. The clashing of swords and confused voices are heard from the other ship, which cannot be seen because of the sail.*

Forgael [*who has remained at the tiller*]. There! there! They come! Gull, gannet, or diver,
But with a man's head, or a fair woman's.
They hover over the masthead awhile
To wait their friends, but when their friends have come
They'll fly upon that secret way of theirs,
One—and one—a couple—five together.
And now they all wheel suddenly and fly
To the other side, and higher in the air,
They've gone up thither, friend's run up by friend;
They've gone to their beloved ones in the air,

In the waste of the high air, that they may wander
Among the windy meadows of the dawn.
But why are they still waiting? Why are they
Circling and circling over the masthead?
Ah! now they all look down—they'll speak of me
What the Ever-living put into their minds,
And of that shadowless unearthly woman
At the world's end. I hear the message now,
But it's all mystery. There's one that cries,
'From love and hate'. Before the sentence ends
Another breaks upon it with a cry,
'From love and death and out of sleep and waking'.
And with the cry another cry is mixed,
'What can we do, being shadows?' All mystery,
And I am drunken with a dizzy light.
But why do they still hover overhead?
Why are you circling there? Why do you linger?
Why do you not run to your desire,
Now that you have happy winged bodies?
Being too busy in the air, and the high air,
They cannot hear my voice. But why that circling?
          [*The Sailors have returned. Dectora is with them.*
[*Turning and seeing her.*] Why are you standing with
          your eyes upon me?
You are not the world's core. O no, no, no!
That cannot be the meaning of the birds.
You are not its core. My teeth are in the world,
But have not bitten yet.

Dectora.   I am a queen,
          And ask for satisfaction upon these
          Who have slain my husband and laid hands upon me.

Forgael. I'd set my hopes on one that had no shadow:—

Where do you come from? who brought you to this
    place?
Why do you cast a shadow? Answer me that.

Dectora. Would that the storm that overthrew my ships,
  And drowned the treasures of nine conquered nations,
  And blew me hither to my lasting sorrow,
  Had drowned me also. But, being yet alive,
  I ask a fitting punishment for all
  That raised their hands against him.

Forgael.   There are some
  That weigh and measure all in these waste seas—
  They that have all the wisdom that's in life,
  And all that prophesying images
  Made of dim gold rave out in secret tombs;
  They have it that the plans of kings and queens
  Are dust on the moth's wing; that nothing matters
  But laughter and tears—laughter, laughter and tears—
  That every man should carry his own soul
  Upon his shoulders.

Dectora.   You've nothing but wild words,
  And I would know if you would give me vengeance.

Forgael. When she finds out that I'll not let her go—
  When she knows that.

Dectora.   What is that you are muttering?
  That you'll not let me go? I am a queen.

Forgael. Although you are more beautiful than any,
  I almost long that it were possible;
  But if I were to put you on that ship,
  With sailors that were sworn to do your will,
  And you had spread a sail for home, a wind

Would rise of a sudden, or a wave so huge
It had washed among the stars and put them out,
And beat the bulwark of your ship on mine,
Until you stood before me on the deck—
As now.

Dectora.   Has wandering in these desolate seas
And listening to the cry of wind and wave
Driven you mad?

Forgael.   But, queen, I am not mad.

Dectora. And yet you say the water and the wind
Would rise against me.

Forgael.   No, I am not mad—
If it be not that hearing messages
From lasting watchers that outlive the moon
At the most quiet midnight is to be stricken.

Dectora. And did those watchers bid you take me
captive?

Forgael. Both you and I are taken in the net.
It was their hands that plucked the winds awake
And blew you hither; and their mouths have
promised
I shall have love in their immortal fashion.
They gave me that old harp of the nine spells
That is more mighty than the sun and moon,
Or than the shivering casting-net of the stars,
That none might take you from me.

Dectora [*first trembling back from the mast where the harp is,*
         and then laughing].   For a moment
Your raving of a message and a harp

More mighty than the stars half troubled me.
But all that's raving. Who is there can compel
The daughter and granddaughter of a king
To be his bedfellow?

Forgael.   Until your lips
Have called me their beloved, I'll not kiss them.

Dectora. My husband and my king died at my feet,
And yet you talk of love.

Forgael.   The movement of time
Is shaken in these seas, and what one does
One moment has no might upon the moment
That follows after.

Dectora.   I understand you now.
You have a Druid craft of wicked music,
Wrung from the cold women of the sea—
A magic that can call a demon up,
Until my body give you kiss for kiss.

Forgael. Your soul shall give the kiss.

Dectora.   I am not afraid
While there's a rope to run into a noose
Or wave to drown. But I have done with words,
And I would have you look into my face
And know that it is fearless.

Forgael.   Do what you will,
For neither I nor you can break a mesh
Of the great golden net that is about us.

Dectora. There's nothing in the world that's worth a
    fear.
    [*She passes Forgael and stands for a moment looking into
    his face.*

I have good reason for that thought.
> [*She runs suddenly on to the raised part of the poop.*
>   And now
I can put fear away as a queen should.
> [*She mounts on the bulwark, and turns towards Forgael.*
Fool, fool! Although you have looked into my face
You did not see my purpose. I shall have gone
Before a hand can touch me.

Forgael [*folding his arms*].   My hands are still;
The Ever-living hold us. Do what you will,
You cannot leap out of the golden net.

First Sailor. There is no need for you to drown. Give
us our pardon and we will bring you home on your
own ship, and make an end of this man that is leading
us to death.

Dectora. I promise it.

Aibric.   I stand upon his side.
I'd strike a blow for him to give him time
To cast his dreams away.

First Sailor. He has put a sudden darkness over the
moon.

Dectora. Nine swords with handles of rhinoceros horn
To him that strikes him first!

First Sailor. I will strike him first. No! for that music
of his might put a beast's head upon my shoulders,
or it may be two heads and they devouring one
another.

Dectora. I'll give a golden galley full of fruit
That has the heady flavour of new wine
To him that wounds him to the death.

First Sailor. I'll strike at him. His spells, when he dies,
will die with him and vanish away.

Second Sailor. I'll strike at him.

The Others.   And I! And I! And I!
                                   [*Forgael plays upon the harp.*

First Sailor [*falling into a dream*]. It is what they are
saying, there is some person dead in the other ship;
we have to go and wake him. They did not say what
way he came to his end, but it was sudden.

Second Sailor. You are right, you are right. We have to
go to that wake.

Dectora. He has flung a Druid spell upon the air,
And set you dreaming.

Second Sailor. What way can we raise a keen, not knowing what name to call him by?

First Sailor. Come on to his ship. His name will come
to mind in a moment. All I know is he died a
thousand years ago, and was never yet waked.

Second Sailor. How can we wake him having no ale?

First Sailor. I saw a skin of ale aboard her—a pigskin
of brown ale.

Third Sailor. Come to the ale, a pigskin of brown ale,
a goatskin of yellow!

First Sailor [*singing*]. Brown ale and yellow; yellow and
brown ale; a goatskin of yellow!

All [*singing*]. Brown ale and yellow; yellow and brown
ale!   [*Sailors go out.*

Dectora. Protect me now, gods that my people swear by!
     [*Aibric has risen from the ground where he had fallen.
     He has begun looking for his sword as if in a dream.*

Aibric. Where is my sword that fell out of my hand
   When I first heard the news? Ah, there it is!
   [*He goes dreamily towards the sword, but Dectora runs
   at it and takes it up before he can reach it.*
   [*Sleepily.*] Queen, give it me.

Dectora.   No, I have need of it.

Aibric. Why do you need a sword? But you may keep it.
   Now that he's dead I have no need of it,
   For everything is gone.

A Sailor [*calling from the other ship*]. Come hither, Aibric,
   And tell me who it is that we are waking.

Aibric [*half to Dectora, half to himself*]. What name had
   that dead king? Arthur of Britain?
   No, no—not Arthur. I remember now.
   It was golden-armed Iollan, and he died
   Broken-hearted, having lost his queen
   Through wicked spells. That is not all the tale,
   For he was killed. O! O! O! O! O! O!
   For golden-armed Iollan has been killed.
   [*He goes out. While he has been speaking, and through
   part of what follows, one hears the singing of the Sailors
   from the other ship. Dectora stands with the sword
   lifted in front of Forgael. He changes the tune.*

Dectora. I will end all your magic on the instant.
   [*Her voice becomes dreamy, and she lowers the sword
   slowly, and finally lets it fall. She spreads out her hair.
   She takes off her crown and lays it upon the deck.*
   The sword is to lie beside him in the grave.
   It was in all his battles. I will spread my hair,
   And wring my hands, and wail him bitterly,

For I have heard that he was proud and laughing,
Blue-eyed, and a quick runner on bare feet,
And that he died a thousand years ago.
O! O! O! O!

              [*Forgael changes the tune*]
          But no, that is not it.
I knew him well, and while I heard him laughing
They killed him at my feet. O! O! O! O!
For golden-armed Iollan that I loved.
But what is it that made me say I loved him?
It was that harper put it in my thoughts,
But it is true. Why did they run upon him,
And beat the golden helmet with their swords?

Forgael. Do you not know me, lady? I am he
  That you are weeping for.

Dectora.   No, for he is dead.
  O! O! O! O! for golden-armed Iollan.

Forgael. It was so given out, but I will prove
  That the grave-diggers in a dreamy frenzy
  Have buried nothing but my golden arms.
  Listen to that low-laughing string of the moon
  And you will recollect my face and voice,
  For you have listened to me playing it
  These thousand years.

    [*He starts up, listening to the birds. The harp slips from
      his hands, and remains leaning against the bulwarks
      behind him.*

                 What are the birds at there?
Why are they all a-flutter of a sudden?
What are you calling out above the mast?
If railing and reproach and mockery
Because I have awakened her to love

N

By magic strings, I'll make this answer to it:
Being driven on by voices and by dreams
That were clear messages from the Ever-living,
I have done right. What could I but obey?
And yet you make a clamour of reproach.

Dectora [*laughing*]. Why, it's a wonder out of reckoning
That I should keen him from the full of the moon
To the horn, and he be hale and hearty.

Forgael. How have I wronged her now that she is
merry?
But no, no, no! your cry is not against me.
You know the councils of the Ever-living,
And all the tossing of your wings is joy,
And all that murmuring's but a marriage song;
But if it be reproach, I answer this:
There is not one among you that made love
By any other means. You call it passion,
Consideration, generosity;
But it was all deceit, and flattery
To win a woman in her own despite,
For love is war, and there is hatred in it;
And if you say that she came willingly—

Dectora. Why do you turn away and hide your face
That I would look upon for ever?

Forgael.   My grief!

Dectora. Have I not loved you for a thousand years?

Forgael. I never have been golden-armed Iollan.

Dectora. I do not understand. I know your face
Better than my own hands.

Forgael.   I have deceived you
Out of all reckoning.

Dectora.   Is it not true
That you were born a thousand years ago,
In islands where the children of Aengus wind
In happy dances under a windy moon,
And that you'll bring me there?

Forgael.   I have deceived you;
I have deceived you utterly.

Dectora.   How can that be?
Is it that though your eyes are full of love
Some other woman has a claim on you,
And I've but half?

Forgael.   O no!

Dectora.   And if there is,
If there be half a hundred more, what matter?
I'll never give another thought to it;
No, no, nor half a thought; but do not speak.
Women are hard and proud and stubborn-hearted,
Their heads being turned with praise and flattery;
And that is why their lovers are afraid
To tell them a plain story.

Forgael.   That's not the story;
But I have done so great a wrong against you,
There is no measure that it would not burst.
I will confess it all.

Dectora.   What do I care,
Now that my body has begun to dream,
And you have grown to be a burning coal
In the imagination and intellect?
If something that's most fabulous were true—
If you had taken me by magic spells,
And killed a lover or husband at my feet—

I would not let you speak, for I would know
That it was yesterday and not to-day
I loved him; I would cover up my ears,
As I am doing now. [*A pause.*] Why do you weep?

Forgael. I weep because I've nothing for your eyes
  But desolate waters and a battered ship.

Dectora. O, why do you not lift your eyes to mine?

Forgael. I weep—I weep because bare night's above,
  And not a roof of ivory and gold.

Dectora. I would grow jealous of the ivory roof,
  And strike the golden pillars with my hands.
  I would that there was nothing in the world
  But my beloved—that night and day had perished,
  And all that is and all that is to be,
  And all that is not the meeting of our lips.

Forgael. Why do you turn your eyes upon bare night?
  Am I to fear the waves, or is the moon
  My enemy?

Dectora.   I looked upon the moon,
  Longing to knead and pull it into shape
  That I might lay it on your head as a crown.
  But now it is your thoughts that wander away,
  For you are looking at the sea. Do you not know
  How great a wrong it is to let one's thought
  Wander a moment when one is in love?
    [*He has moved away. She follows him. He is looking out
      over the sea, shading his eyes.*
  Why are you looking at the sea?

Forgael.   Look there!
  There where the cloud creeps up upon the moon.

Dectora. What is there but a troop of ash-grey birds
  That fly into the west?
    [*The scene darkens, but there is a ray of light upon the
    figures.*

Forgael.   But listen, listen!

Dectora. What is there but the crying of the birds?

Forgael. If you'll but listen closely to that crying
  You'll hear them calling out to one another
  With human voices.

Dectora.   Clouds have hid the moon.
  The birds cry out, what can I do but tremble?

Forgael. They have been circling over our heads in the
      air,
  But now that they have taken to the road
  We have to follow, for they are our pilots;
  They're crying out. Can you not hear their cry?—
  'There is a country at the end of the world
  Where no child's born but to outlive the moon.'
    [*The Sailors come in with Aibric. They carry torches.*

Aibric. We have lit upon a treasure that's so great
  Imagination cannot reckon it.
  The hold is full—boxes of precious spice,
  Ivory images with amethyst eyes,
  Dragons with eyes of ruby. The whole ship
  Flashes as if it were a net of herrings.
  Let us return to our own country, Forgael,
  And spend it there. Have you not found this queen?
  What more have you to look for on the seas?

Forgael. I cannot—I am going on to the end.
  As for this woman, I think she is coming with me.

Aibric. Speak to him, lady, and bid him turn the ship.

He knows that he is taking you to death;
He cannot contradict me.

Dectora.   Is that true?

Forgael. I do not know for certain.

Dectora.   Carry me
To some sure country, some familiar place.
Have we not everything that life can give
In having one another?

Forgael.   How could I rest
If I refused the messengers and pilots
With all those sights and all that crying out?

Dectora. I am a woman, I die at every breath.

Aibric [to the Sailors]. To the other ship, for there's no
     help in words.
And I will follow you and cut the rope
When I have said farewell to this man here,
For neither I nor any living man
Will look upon his face again.
     [Sailors go out, leaving one torch perhaps in a torch-
     holder on the bulwark.

Forgael [to Dectora].   Go with him,
For he will shelter you and bring you home.

Aibric [taking Forgael's hand]. I'll do it for his sake.

Dectora.   No. Take this sword
And cut the rope, for I go on with Forgael.

Aibric. Farewell! Farewell!
                    [He goes out. The light grows stronger.

Dectora.   The sword is in the rope—
The rope's in two—it falls into the sea,
It whirls into the foam. O ancient worm,

Dragon that loved the world and held us to it,
You are broken, you are broken. The world drifts
    away,
And I am left alone with my beloved,
Who cannot put me from his sight for ever.
We are alone for ever, and I laugh,
Forgael, because you cannot put me from you.
The mist has covered the heavens, and you and I
Shall be alone for ever. We two—this crown—
I half remember. It has been in my dreams.
Bend lower, O king, that I may crown you with it.
O flower of the branch, O bird among the leaves,
O silver fish that my two hands have taken
Out of the running stream, O morning star,
Trembling in the blue heavens like a white fawn
Upon the misty border of the wood,
Bend lower, that I may cover you with my hair,
For we will gaze upon this world no longer.
                    [*The harp begins to burn as with fire.*

Forgael [*gathering Dectora's hair about him*]. Beloved, hav-
    ing dragged the net about us,
And knitted mesh to mesh, we grow immortal;
And that old harp awakens of itself
To cry aloud to the grey birds, and dreams,
That have had dreams for father, live in us.

                    THE END

THE WORDS UPON THE
WINDOW-PANE

1934

IN MEMORY OF
LADY GREGORY
IN WHOSE HOUSE IT WAS WRITTEN

THE WORDS UPON THE WINDOW-PANE

PERSONS IN THE PLAY

Dr. Trench	Cornelius Patterson
Miss Mackenna	Abraham Johnson
John Corbet	Mrs. Mallet

Mrs. Henderson

A lodging-house room, an armchair, a little table in front of it, chairs on either side. A fireplace and window. A kettle on the hob and some tea-things on a dresser. A door to back and towards the right. Through the door one can see an entrance hall. The sound of a knocker. Miss Mackenna passes through and then she re-enters hall together with John Corbet, a man of twenty-two or twenty-three, and Dr. Trench, a man of between sixty and seventy.

Dr. Trench [*in hall*]. May I introduce John Corbet, one of the Corbets of Ballymoney, but at present a Cambridge student? This is Miss Mackenna, our enthusiastic secretary. [*They come into room, take off their coats.*]

Miss Mackenna. I thought it better to let you in myself. This country is still sufficiently medieval to make spiritualism an undesirable theme for gossip. Give me your coats and hats, I will put them in my own room. It is just across the hall. Better sit down, your watches must be fast. Mrs. Henderson is lying down, as she always does before a séance. We won't begin for ten minutes yet. [*She goes out with hats and coats.*]

Dr. Trench. Miss Mackenna does all the real work of the Dublin Spiritualists' Association. She did all the correspondence with Mrs. Henderson, and persuaded the landlady to let her this big room and a small room upstairs. We are a poor society and could not guarantee anything in advance. Mrs. Henderson has come from London at her own risk. She was born in Dublin and wants to spread the movement here. She lives very economically and does not expect a great deal. We all give what we can. A poor woman with the soul of an apostle.

John Corbet. Have there been many séances?

Dr. Trench. Only three so far.

John Corbet. I hope she will not mind my scepticism. I have looked into Myers' *Human Personality* and a wild book by Conan Doyle, but am unconvinced.

Dr. Trench. We all have to find the truth for ourselves. Lord Dunraven, then Lord Adare, introduced my father to the famous David Home. My father often told me that he saw David Home floating in the air in broad daylight, but I did not believe a word of it. I had to investigate for myself, and I was very hard to convince. Mrs. Piper, an American trance medium, not unlike Mrs. Henderson, convinced me.

John Corbet. A state of somnambulism and voices coming through her lips that purport to be those of dead persons?

Dr. Trench. Exactly: quite the best kind of mediumship if you want to establish the identity of a spirit. But do not expect too much. There has been a hostile influence.

John Corbet. You mean an evil spirit?

Dr. Trench. The poet Blake said that he never knew a bad man that had not something very good about him. I say a hostile influence, an influence that disturbed the last séance very seriously. I cannot tell you what happened, for I have not been at any of Mrs. Henderson's séances. Trance mediumship has nothing new to show me—I told the young people when they made me their President that I would probably stay at home, that I could get more out of Emanuel Swedenborg than out of any séance. [*A knock.*] That is probably old Cornelius Patterson; he thinks they race horses and whippets in the other world, and is, so they tell me, so anxious to find out if he is right that he is always punctual. Miss Mackenna will keep him to herself for some minutes. He gives her tips for Harold's Cross.

[*Miss Mackenna crosses to hall door and admits Cornelius Patterson. She brings him to her room across the hall.*

John Corbet [*who has been wandering about*]. This is a wonderful room for a lodging-house.

Dr. Trench. It was a private house until about fifty years ago. It was not so near the town in those days, and there are large stables at the back. Quite a number of notable people lived here. Grattan was born upstairs—no, not Grattan, Curran perhaps—I forget—but I do know that this house in the early part of the eighteenth century belonged to friends of Jonathan Swift, or rather of Stella. Swift chaffed her in the *Journal to Stella* because of certain small sums of money she lost at cards probably in this very room.

That was before Vanessa appeared upon the scene. It was a country house in those days, surrounded by trees and gardens. Somebody cut some lines from a poem of hers upon the window-pane—tradition says Stella herself. [*A knock.*] Here they are, but you will hardly make them out in this light. [*They stand in the window. Corbet stoops down to see better. Miss Mackenna and Abraham Johnson enter and stand near door.*]

Abraham Johnson. Where is Mrs. Henderson?

Miss Mackenna. She is upstairs; she always rests before a séance.

Abraham Johnson. I must see her before the séance. I know exactly what to do to get rid of this evil influence.

Miss Mackenna. If you go up to see her there will be no séance at all. She says it is dangerous even to think, much less to speak of, an evil influence.

Abraham Johnson. Then I shall speak to the President.

Miss Mackenna. Better talk the whole thing over first in my room. Mrs. Henderson says that there must be perfect harmony.

Abraham Johnson. Something must be done. The last séance was completely spoiled. [*A knock.*]

Miss Mackenna. That may be Mrs. Mallet; she is a very experienced spiritualist. Come to my room, old Patterson and some others are there already. [*She brings him to the other room and later crosses to hall door to admit Mrs. Mallet.*]

John Corbet. I know those lines well—they are part of a poem Stella wrote for Swift's fifty-fourth birthday.

Only three poems of hers and some lines she added to a poem of Swift's have come down to us, but they are enough to prove her a better poet than Swift. Even those few words on the window make me think of a seventeenth-century poet, Donne or Crashaw. [*He quotes*]

'You taught how I might youth prolong
By knowing what is right and wrong,
How from my heart to bring supplies
Of lustre to my fading eyes.'

How strange that a celibate scholar, well on in life, should keep the love of two such women! He met Vanessa in London at the height of his political power. She followed him to Dublin. She loved him for nine years, perhaps died of love, but Stella loved him all her life.

Dr. Trench. I have shown that writing to several persons and you are the first who has recognised the lines.

John Corbet. I am writing an essay on Swift and Stella for my doctorate at Cambridge. I hope to prove that in Swift's day men of intellect reached the height of their power—the greatest position they ever attained in society and the State, that everything great in Ireland and in our character, in what remains of our architecture, comes from that day; that we have kept its seal longer than England.

Dr. Trench. A tragic life: Bolingbroke, Harley, Ormonde, all those great Ministers that were his friends, banished and broken.

John Corbet. I do not think you can explain him in that way—his tragedy had deeper foundations, his ideal order was the Roman Senate, his ideal men Brutus and Cato. Such an order and such men had seemed possible once more, but the movement passed and he foresaw the ruin to come, Democracy, Rousseau, the French Revolution; that is why he hated the common run of men—'I hate lawyers, I hate doctors,' he said, 'though I love Dr. So-and-so and Judge So-and so'—that is why he wrote *Gulliver*, that is why he wore out his brain, that is why he felt *saeva indignatio*, that is why he sleeps under the greatest epitaph in history. You remember how it goes? It is almost finer in English than in Latin: 'He has gone where fierce indignation can lacerate his heart no more.'

[*Abraham Johnson comes in, followed by Mrs. Mallet and Cornelius Patterson.*

Abraham Johnson. Something must be done, Dr. Trench, to drive away the influence that has destroyed our séances. I have come here week after week at considerable expense. I am from Belfast. I am by profession a minister of the Gospel, I do a great deal of work among the poor and ignorant. I produce considerable effect by singing and preaching, but I know that my effect should be much greater than it is. My hope is that I shall be able to communicate with the great Evangelist Sankey. I want to ask him to stand invisible beside me when I speak or sing, and lay his hands upon my head and give me such a portion of his power that my work may be blessed as the work of Moody and Sankey was blessed.

Mrs. Mallet. What Mr. Johnson says about the hostile influence is quite true. The last two séances were completely spoilt. I am thinking of starting a teashop in Folkestone. I followed Mrs. Henderson to Dublin to get my husband's advice, but two spirits kept talking and would not let any other spirit say a word.

Dr. Trench. Did the spirits say the same thing and go through the same drama at both séances?

Mrs. Mallet. Yes—just as if they were characters in some kind of horrible play.

Dr. Trench. That is what I was afraid of.

Mrs. Mallet. My husband was drowned at sea ten years ago, but constantly speaks to me through Mrs. Henderson as if he were still alive. He advises me about everything I do, and I am utterly lost if I cannot question him.

Cornelius Patterson. I never did like the Heaven they talk about in churches: but when somebody told me that Mrs. Mallet's husband ate and drank and went about with his favourite dog, I said to myself, 'That is the place for Corney Patterson'. I came here to find out if it was true, and I declare to God I have not heard one word about it.

Abraham Johnson. I ask you, Dr. Trench, as President of the Dublin Spiritualists' Association, to permit me to read the ritual of exorcism appointed for such occasions. After the last séance I copied it out of an old book in the library of Belfast University. I have it here. [*He takes paper out of his pocket.*

Dr. Trench. The spirits are people like ourselves, we treat them as our guests and protect them from discourtesy and violence, and every exorcism is a curse or a threatened curse. We do not admit that there are

O

evil spirits. Some spirits are earth-bound—they think they are still living and go over and over some action of their past lives, just as we go over and over some painful thought, except that where they are thought is reality. For instance, when a spirit which has died a violent death comes to a medium for the first time, it re-lives all the pains of death.

Mrs. Mallet. When my husband came for the first time the medium gasped and struggled as if she was drowning. It was terrible to watch.

Dr. Trench. Sometimes a spirit re-lives not the pain of death but some passionate or tragic moment of life. Swedenborg describes this and gives the reason for it. There is an incident of the kind in the *Odyssey*, and many in Eastern literature; the murderer repeats his murder, the robber his robbery, the lover his serenade, the soldier hears the trumpet once again. If I were a Catholic I would say that such spirits were in Purgatory. In vain do we write *requiescat in pace* upon the tomb, for they must suffer, and we in our turn must suffer until God gives peace. Such spirits do not often come to séances unless those séances are held in houses where those spirits lived, or where the event took place. This spirit which speaks those incomprehensible words and does not answer when spoken to is of such a nature. The more patient we are, the more quickly will it pass out of its passion and its remorse.

Abraham Johnson. I am still convinced that the spirit which disturbed the last séance is evil. If I may not exorcise it I will certainly pray for protection.

Dr. Trench. Mrs. Henderson's control, Lulu, is able and experienced and can protect both medium and sitters, but it may help Lulu if you pray that the spirit find rest.

[*Abraham Johnson sits down and prays silently, moving his lips. Mrs. Henderson comes in with Miss Mackenna and others. Miss Mackenna shuts the door.*

Dr. Trench. Mrs. Henderson, may I introduce to you Mr. Corbet, a young man from Cambridge and a sceptic, who hopes that you will be able to convince him.

Mrs. Henderson. We were all sceptics once. He must not expect too much from a first séance. He must persevere. [*She sits in the armchair and the others begin to seat themselves. Miss Mackenna goes to John Corbet and they remain standing.*]

Miss Mackenna. I am glad that you are a sceptic.

John Corbet. I thought you were a spiritualist.

Miss Mackenna. I have seen a good many séances, and sometimes think it is all coincidence and thought-transference. [*She says this in a low voice.*] Then at other times I think as Dr. Trench does, and then I feel like Job—you know the quotation—the hair of my head stands up. A spirit passes before my face.

Mrs. Mallet. Turn the key, Dr. Trench, we don't want anybody blundering in here. [*Dr. Trench locks door.*] Come and sit here, Miss Mackenna.

Miss Mackenna. No, I am going to sit beside Mr. Corbet.
[*Corbet and Miss Mackenna sit down.*

John Corbet. You feel like Job to-night?

Miss Mackenna. I feel that something is going to happen, that is why I am glad that you are a sceptic.

John Corbet. You feel safer?

Miss Mackenna. Yes, safer.

Mrs. Henderson. I am glad to meet all my dear friends again and to welcome Mr. Corbet amongst us. As he is a stranger I must explain that we do not call up spirits, we make the right conditions and they come. I do not know who is going to come; sometimes there are a great many and the guides choose between them. The guides try to send somebody for everybody but do not always succeed. If you want to speak to some dear friend who has passed over, do not be discouraged. If your friend cannot come this time, maybe he can next time. My control is a dear little girl called Lulu who died when she was five or six years old. She describes the spirits present and tells us what spirit wants to speak. Miss Mackenna, a verse of a hymn, please, the same we had last time, and will everyone join in the singing.

[*They sing the following lines from Hymn 564, Dublin Church Hymnal.*

'Sun of my soul, Thou Saviour dear,
It is not night if Thou be near:
O may no earth-born cloud arise
To hide Thee from Thy servant's eyes.'

[*Mrs. Henderson is leaning back in her chair asleep.*

Miss Mackenna [*to John Corbet*]. She always snores like that when she is going off.

Mrs. Henderson [*in a child's voice*]. Lulu so glad to see all her friends.

Mrs. Mallet. And we are glad you have come, Lulu.

Mrs. Henderson [*in a child's voice*]. Lulu glad to see new friend.

Miss Mackenna [*to John Corbet*]. She is speaking to you.

John Corbet. Thank you, Lulu.

Mrs. Henderson [*in a child's voice*]. You mustn't laugh at the way I talk.

John Corbet. I am not laughing, Lulu.

Mrs. Henderson [*in a child's voice*]. Nobody must laugh. Lulu does her best but can't say big long words. Lulu sees a tall man here, lots of hair on face [*Mrs. Henderson passes her hands over her cheeks and chin*], not much on the top of his head [*Mrs. Henderson passes her hand over the top of her head*], red necktie, and such a funny sort of pin.

Mrs. Mallet. Yes. . . . Yes. . . .

Mrs. Henderson [*in a child's voice*]. Pin like a horseshoe.

Mrs. Mallet. It's my husband.

Mrs. Henderson [*in a child's voice*]. He has a message.

Mrs. Mallet. Yes.

Mrs. Henderson [*in a child's voice*]. Lulu cannot hear. He is too far off. He has come near. Lulu can hear now. He says . . . he says, 'Drive that man away!' He is pointing to somebody in the corner, that corner over there. He says it is the bad man who spoilt everything last time. If they won't drive him away, Lulu will scream.

Miss Mackenna. That horrible spirit again.

Abraham Johnson. Last time he monopolised the séance.

Mrs. Mallet. He would not let anybody speak but himself.

Mrs. Henderson [*in a child's voice*]. They have driven that bad man away. Lulu sees a young lady.

Mrs. Mallet. Is not my husband here?

Mrs. Henderson [*in a child's voice*]. Man with funny pin gone away. Young lady here—Lulu thinks she must be at a fancy dress party, such funny clothes, hair all in curls—all bent down on floor near that old man with glasses.

Dr. Trench. No, I do not recognize her.

Mrs. Henderson [*in a child's voice*]. That bad man, that bad old man in the corner, they have let him come back. Lulu is going to scream. O. . . . O. . . . [*In a man's voice*]. How dare you write to her? How dare you ask if we were married? How dare you question her?

Dr. Trench. A soul in its agony—it cannot see us or hear us.

Mrs. Henderson [*upright and rigid, only her lips moving, and still in a man's voice*]. You sit crouching there. Did you not hear what I said? How dared you question her? I found you an ignorant little girl without intellect, without moral ambition. How many times did I not stay away from great men's houses, how many times forsake the Lord Treasurer, how many times neglect the business of the State that we might read Plutarch together?

  [*Abraham Johnson half rises. Dr. Trench motions him to remain seated.*

Dr. Trench. Silence!

Abraham Johnson. But, Dr. Trench . . .

Dr. Trench. Hush—we can do nothing.

Mrs. Henderson [*speaking as before*]. I taught you to think in every situation of life not as Hester Vanhomrigh would think in that situation, but as Cato or Brutus would, and now you behave like some common slut with her ear against the keyhole.

John Corbet [*to Miss Mackenna*]. It is Swift, Jonathan Swift, talking to the woman he called Vanessa. She was christened Hester Vanhomrigh.

Mrs. Henderson [*in Vanessa's voice*]. I questioned her, Jonathan, because I love. Why have you let me spend hours in your company if you did not want me to love you? [*In Swift's voice.*] When I re-built Rome in your mind it was as though I walked its streets. [*In Vanessa's voice.*] Was that all, Jonathan? Was I nothing but a painter's canvas? [*In Swift's voice.*] My God, do you think it was easy? I was a man of strong passions and I had sworn never to marry. [*In Vanessa's voice.*] If you and she are not married, why should we not marry like other men and women? I loved you from the first moment when you came to my mother's house and began to teach me. I thought it would be enough to look at you, to speak to you, to hear you speak. I followed you to Ireland five years ago and I can bear it no longer. It is not enough to look, to speak, to hear. Jonathan, Jonathan, I am a woman, the women Brutus and Cato loved were not different. [*In Swift's voice.*] I have something in my blood that no child must inherit. I have constant attacks of dizziness; I pretend they come from a surfeit of fruit when I was a child. I had them in London . . . there was a great doctor there, Dr. Arbuthnot, I told him of those attacks of dizziness, I told him of worse things. It was he who explained. There is a line of Dryden's. . . . [*In Vanessa's voice.*] O, I know—'Great wits are sure to madness near allied'. If you had children, Jonathan, my blood would make them healthy. I will take your hand, I will lay it upon my heart—upon the Vanhomrigh blood that has been healthy for generations. [*Mrs. Henderson slowly raises her left hand.*] That is the first time you have touched my body, Jonathan. [*Mrs. Henderson stands up and remains rigid. In Swift's voice.*] What do I care if it be healthy? What do I care if it could make mine healthy? Am I to add another to the healthy rascaldom and knavery of the world? [*In Vanessa's voice.*] Look at me, Jonathan. Your arrogant intellect separates us. Give me both your hands. I will put them upon my breast. [*Mrs. Henderson raises her right hand to the level of her left and then raises both to her breast.*] O, it is white—white as the gambler's dice—white ivory dice. Think of the uncertainty. Perhaps a mad child—perhaps a rascal—Perhaps a knave—perhaps not, Jonathan. The dice of the intellect are loaded, but I am the common ivory dice. [*Her hands are stretched out as though drawing somebody towards her.*] It is not my hands that draw you back. My hands are weak, they could not draw you back if you did not love as I love. You said that you have strong passions; that is true, Jonathan—no man in Ireland is so passionate. That is why you need me, that is why you need children, nobody has greater need. You are growing old. An old man without children is very solitary. Even his friends, men as old as he, turn away, they turn towards the young, their children or their children's children. They cannot endure an old man like themselves. [*Mrs. Henderson moves away from the chair, her movements gradually growing convulsive.*] You are not too old for the dice, Jonathan, but a few years if you turn away will make you an old miserable childless man. [*In Swift's voice.*] O God, hear the prayer of Jonathan Swift, that afflicted man, and grant that he may leave to posterity nothing but his intellect that came to him from Heaven. [*In Vanessa's voice.*] Can you face solitude with that mind, Jonathan? [*Mrs. Henderson goes to the door, finds that it is closed.*] Dice, white ivory dice. [*In Swift's voice.*] My God, I am left alone with my enemy. Who locked the door, who locked me in with my enemy? [*Mrs. Henderson beats upon the door, sinks to the floor and then speaks as Lulu.*] Bad old man! Do not let him come back. Bad old man does not know he is dead. Lulu cannot find fathers, mothers, sons that have passed over. Power almost gone. [*Mrs. Mallet leads Mrs. Henderson, who seems very exhausted, back to her chair. She is still asleep. She speaks again as Lulu.*] Another verse of hymn. Everybody sing. Hymn will bring good influence.

[*They sing*]

'If some poor wandering child of Thine
 Have spurned to-day the voice divine,
 Now, Lord, the gracious work begin;
 Let him no more lie down in sin.'

[*During the hymn Mrs. Henderson has been murmuring 'Stella', but the singing has almost drowned her voice. The singers draw one another's attention to the fact that she is speaking. The singing stops.*]

Dr. Trench. I thought she was speaking.

Mrs. Mallet. I saw her lips move.

Dr. Trench. She would be more comfortable with a cushion, but we might wake her.

Mrs. Mallet. Nothing can wake her out of a trance like that until she wakes up herself. [*She brings a cushion and she and Dr. Trench put Mrs. Henderson into a more comfortable position.*]

Mrs. Henderson [*in Swift's voice*]. Stella.

Miss Mackenna [*to John Corbet*]. Did you hear that? She said 'Stella'.

John Corbet. Vanessa has gone, Stella has taken her place.

Miss Mackenna. Did you notice the change while we were singing? The new influence in the room?

John Corbet. I thought I did, but it must have been fancy.

Mrs. Mallet. Hush!

Mrs. Henderson [*in Swift's voice*]. Have I wronged you, beloved Stella? Are you unhappy? You have no children, you have no lover, you have no husband. A cross and ageing man for friend—nothing but that. But no, do not answer—you have answered already in that poem you wrote for my last birthday. With what scorn you speak of the common lot of women 'with no adornment but a face—

> 'Before the thirtieth year of life
> A maid forlorn or hated wife.'

It is the thought of the great Chrysostom who wrote in a famous passage that women loved according to the soul, loved as saints can love, keep their beauty longer, have greater happiness than women loved according to the flesh. That thought has comforted me, but it is a terrible thing to be responsible for another's happiness. There are moments when I doubt, when I think Chrysostom may have been wrong. But now I have your poem to drive doubt away. You have addressed me in these noble words:

> 'You taught how I might youth prolong
> By knowing what is right and wrong;
> How from my heart to bring supplies
> Of lustre to my fading eyes;
> How soon a beauteous mind repairs
> The loss of chang'd or falling hairs;
> How wit and virtue from within
> Can spread a smoothness o'er the skin.'

John Corbet. The words upon the window-pane!

Mrs. Henderson [*in Swift's voice*]. Then, because you understand that I am afraid of solitude, afraid of outliving my friends—and myself—you comfort me in that last verse—you overpraise my moral nature when you attribute to it a rich mantle, but O how touching those words which describe your love:

> 'Late dying, may you cast a shred
> Of that rich mantle o'er my head;
> To bear with dignity my sorrow,
> One day alone, then die to-morrow.'

Yes, you will close my eyes, Stella. O, you will live long after me, dear Stella, for you are still a young woman, but you will close my eyes. [*Mrs. Henderson sinks back in chair and speaks as Lulu.*] Bad old man gone. Power all used up. Lulu can do no more. Good-bye, friends. [*Mrs. Henderson, speaking in her own voice.*] Go away, go away! [*She wakes.*] I saw him a moment ago, has he spoilt the séance again?

Mrs. Mallet. Yes, Mrs. Henderson, my husband came, but he was driven away.

Dr. Trench. Mrs. Henderson is very tired. We must leave her to rest. [*To Mrs. Henderson.*] You did your best and nobody can do more than that. [*He takes out money.*]

Mrs. Henderson. No. . . . No. . . . I cannot take any money, not after a séance like that.

Dr. Trench. Of course you must take it, Mrs. Henderson. [*He puts money on table, and Mrs. Henderson gives a furtive glance to see how much it is. She does the same as each sitter lays down his or her money.*]

Mrs. Mallet. A bad séance is just as exhausting as a good séance, and you must be paid.

Mrs. Henderson. No. . . . No. . . . Please don't. It is very wrong to take money for such a failure.

        [*Mrs. Mallet lays down money.*

Cornelius Patterson. A jockey is paid whether he wins or not. [*He lays down money.*]

Miss Mackenna. That spirit rather thrilled me. [*She lays down money.*]

Mrs. Henderson. If you insist, I must take it.

Abraham Johnson. I shall pray for you to-night. I shall ask God to bless and protect your séances. [*He lays down money.*]

        [*All go out except John Corbet and Mrs. Henderson.*

John Corbet. I know you are tired, Mrs. Henderson, but

I must speak to you. I have been deeply moved by what I have heard. This is my contribution to prove that I am satisfied, completely satisfied. [*He puts a note on the table.*]

Mrs. Henderson. A pound note—nobody ever gives me more than ten shillings, and yet the séance was a failure.

John Corbet [*sitting down near Mrs. Henderson*]. When I say I am satisfied I do not mean that I am convinced it was the work of spirits. I prefer to think that you created it all, that you are an accomplished actress and scholar. In my essay for my Cambridge doctorate I examine all the explanations of Swift's celibacy offered by his biographers and prove that the explanation you selected was the only plausible one. But there is something I must ask you. Swift was the chief representative of the intellect of his epoch, that arrogant intellect free at last from superstition. He foresaw its collapse. He foresaw Democracy, he must have dreaded the future. Did he refuse to beget children because of that dread? Was Swift mad? Or was it the intellect itself that was mad?

Mrs. Henderson. Who are you talking of, sir?

John Corbet. Swift, of course.

Mrs. Henderson. Swift? I do not know anybody called Swift.

John Corbet. Jonathan Swift, whose spirit seemed to be present to-night.

Mrs. Henderson. What? That dirty old man?

John Corbet. He was neither old nor dirty when Stella and Vanessa loved him.

Mrs. Henderson. I saw him very clearly just as I woke up. His clothes were dirty, his face covered with boils. Some disease had made one of his eyes swell up, it stood out from his face like a hen's egg.

John Corbet. He looked like that in his old age. Stella had been dead a long time. His brain had gone, his friends had deserted him. The man appointed to take care of him beat him to keep him quiet.

Mrs. Henderson. Now they are old, now they are young. They change all in a moment as their thought changes. It is sometimes a terrible thing to be out of the body, God help us all.

Dr. Trench [*at doorway*]. Come along, Corbet, Mrs. Henderson is tired out.

John Corbet. Good-bye, Mrs. Henderson. [*He goes out with Dr. Trench. All the sitters except Miss Mackenna, who has returned to her room, pass along the passage on their way to the front door. Mrs. Henderson counts the money, finds her purse, which is in a vase on the mantelpiece, and puts the money in it.*]

Mrs. Henderson. How tired I am! I'd be the better of a cup of tea. [*She finds the teapot and puts kettle on fire, and then as she crouches down by the hearth suddenly lifts up her hands and counting her fingers, speaking in Swift's voice.*] Five great Ministers that were my friends are gone, ten great Ministers that were my friends are gone. I have not fingers enough to count the great Ministers that were my friends and that are gone.

[*She wakes with a start and speaks in her own voice.*]
Where did I put that tea-caddy? Ah! there it is. And
there should be a cup and saucer. [*She finds the saucer.*]
But where's the cup? [*She moves aimlessly about the stage
and then, letting the saucer fall and break, speaks in Swift's
voice.*] Perish the day on which I was born!

THE END

Printed in Great Britain by R. & R. CLARK, LIMITED, *Edinburgh.*